The Three Virtues of Effective Parenting

Advance Praise for *The Three Virtues of Effective Parenting*

Shirley Yuen personally embodies the three virtues she shares with her children and encourages other parents to do the same. Precious treasure comes to those who are willing to take this new and unique path that leads to surprisingly effective results.
—BOBBIE SANDOZ MERRILL, author of *Parachutes for Parents*

Read this book and follow her wise teachings and you will be inspired to be a benevolent parent who will give your children the love and attention they so deserve. This book will open your eyes and your heart and will take you down many paths that you may never have traveled. Author Shirley Yuen will take you on the path that will lead to a healthier family where children are even more valued and even more loved.
—AILEEN DEESE, Executive Director of Prevent Child Abuse Hawaii

There is no single voice that has been more persistent in shaping human culture than that of Confucius, China's preeminent teacher. In this slim yet brimming volume, Shirley Yuen brings the distilled values of the ages to guide us in our awesome, challenging, and sometimes overwhelming responsibility of being effective parents. For China, family has always been the governing metaphor in all aspects of the human experience. Yuen brings tradition and her own personal virtuosity in lived parenting to demonstrate how to grow our family relations, and in so doing, how to enchant the most common yet most valuable business of a human life.
—ROGER T. AMES, Professor of Chinese Philosophy, University of Hawaii

Yuen helps western parents practice the Confucian art of self-cultivation while raising children within the context of Western society. As she describes her mistakes and the work she did to correct them, reminding the reader that "Not correcting a mistake is a mistake" as Confucius said, she gives insight into how she learned to be a better parent with rare honesty and humor. I would heartily recommend this book to prospective parents, parents, and grandparents.
—HELEN P. YOUNG, Associate Scholar, Center for East Asian Studies, Stanford University

The Three Virtues of Effective Parenting

Lessons from Confucius
on the Power of Benevolence,
Wisdom, and Courage

Shirley Yuen

TUTTLE PUBLISHING
Boston · Rutland, Vermont · Tokyo

First published in 2005 by Tuttle Publishing, an imprint of Periplus
Editions (HK) Ltd., with editorial offices at 153 Milk Street, Boston,
Massachusetts 02109.

Grateful acknowledgment is made to the Humanics Publishing Group for
permission to reprint the excerpt on page xiv from *The Way of Virtue* by
James Vollbracht. Copyright © 1998 by James Vollbracht.

Library of Congress Cataloging-in-Publication Data

Yuen, Shirley, 1952-
  The three virtues of effective parenting : lessons from Confucius on the
power of benevolence, wisdom, and courage / Shirley Yuen.
     p. cm.
  Includes bibliographical references and index.
  ISBN 0-8048-3539-X (pbk.)
  1. Philosophy, Confucian. I. Title: The power of benevolence, wisdom,
and courage. II. Title.   B127.C65Y795 2004
  179'.9'085—dc22

                              2004007209

Distributed by

North America, Latin	Japan	Asia Pacific
America & Europe	Tuttle Publishing	Berkeley Books Pte. Ltd.
Tuttle Publishing	Yaekari Building,	130 Joo Seng Road
364 Innovation Drive	3rd Floor	#06-01/03 Olivine Building
North Clarendon, VT	5-4-12 Ōsaki	Singapore 368357
05759-9436	Shinagawa-ku	Tel: (65) 6280-1330
Tel: (802) 773-8930	Tokyo 141 0032	Fax: (65) 6280-6290
Fax: (802) 773-6993	Tel: (03) 5437-0171	inquiries@periplus.com.sg
info@tuttlepublishing.com	Fax: (03) 5437-0755	www.periplus.com
www.tuttlepublishing.com	tuttle-sales@gol.com	

First edition
08 07 06 05 04   10 9 8 7 6 5 4 3 2 1
Cover art: Ta Shan. Collection of Shirley Yuen.
Printed in Canada

DEDICATION

Dedicated with love and gratitude to my mother,
Wong Suk Ying, and my father, Yuen Kong Sang,
whose unconditional love for me had surpassed any
parenting skill that could be learned from books.

CONTENTS

ACKNOWLEDGMENTS

My heartfelt gratitude goes to my literary agent Wendy Keller, who had shared my vision and enthusiasm for this book even before I wrote my book proposal. Thank you so much for helping me in every step along the way.

I am indebted to my editor Jennifer Lantagne, and everyone who helped to shape this book at Tuttle Publishing, for their expertise and kind assistance. Your patience and understanding are greatly appreciated.

My gratitude to all the parenting experts and authors who were at my rescue throughout my parenting journey. Special thanks go to Bobbie Sandoz for teaching me so much about my children and myself. Thank you for being such a wonderful mentor.

This book could not have been possible without Confucius. His timeless insights have transformed me from an anxious and confused parent to one who truly feels the joy and fulfillment of parenthood. *Xie Xie.*

I am also grateful to my ex-husband, Richard Hui, for his encouragement and support from the inception of this book. Your help with my research in Chinese philosophy is greatly appreciated.

Above all, I need to thank God for blessing me with two wonderful children. My son and daughter have helped me to look within myself and learn to become a better person and a better parent. To Eric and Kristy, thank you for showing me how to love and be loved.

Last but not least, my love and gratitude to Penny, my canine friend, who was always by my side while I labored through this book.

PREFACE

I was born and raised in Hong Kong, and have been exposed to the best and worst of both Eastern and Western culture since birth. My cultural identity was further tested when I attended college and then raised my two children in the United States.

At times I feel the conflicts or discontinuities between Eastern and Western philosophies and values. I tend to act like Aristotle in my quest for personal freedom and then think like Confucius in my concern for a more all-embracing harmony in my surroundings. But in a way, these contradictory focuses have helped me appreciate the best of both worlds, and most important of all, they've helped me find balance in the way I respond to what happens around me. Central to my life has been my role as a parent. It is also an arena where I've come to appreciate how much Eastern wisdom and Western parenting can work hand-in-hand.

❖ HOW IT ALL STARTED ❖

The Eastern philosophy and Western Parenting book collection in my house had always been on two different bookshelves. I studied them both carefully. And separately. But I can still remember the day when the wisdom of Confucius came to the rescue when I was desperately looking for help in one of my parenting books.

It was seventeen years ago . . . I was standing in front of my two-and-a-half-year-old son who was having a tantrum. I can't remember what he was refusing to do, but I got very angry because he was demanding that *I* get out of *his* room. I quickly tried to remember what my parenting books said about situations like this but before I could figure out if this was a "tantrum" or "defying behavior," my anger seemed to have set fire to everything that I had learned from all of my parenting books.

I could hear myself yelling as loud, if not louder, than the tiny two-and-a-half-year-old monster in front of me. My heart was beating faster than it does in my aerobics class and for a second, I thought I was going to hit my little boy. Then suddenly, at the very back of my mind, I heard a gentle voice that said, "If a person is filled with anger, he will not be able to behave correctly, for then his mind no longer resides in him. He will look but not see; he will listen but not hear. . . ." (Commentary VII from Confucius' *Doctrine of the Mean*.)

I suddenly stopped yelling. I took my son in my arms and tried to *see* him as a two-and-a-half-year-old. I tried to *hear* what he was really trying to tell me. That was the first time that I took the courage to see what I did not see in *myself*. That was the day that I started to empower myself with the wisdom of Confucius to complement the wisdom of Dr. Spock, Parents Effective Training (P.E.T.), Systematic Training for Effective Parenting (S.T.E.P.) and other Western parenting experts. I started to recognize that it is essential to cultivate virtue if we want to be wise parents who truly care, nurture, and guide our children. It took much learning and thinking to discover that the power of virtue is two-fold: *On one hand, virtue helps us to change ourselves so that we become better people; on the other hand, it helps us influence the behavior of people around us in a positive way.* How I wish I had realized the significance of cultivating both aspects of virtue earlier, for then I would not have struggled with parenting for so many years.

Good parenting skills are important; while some come naturally, others must be learned. In this book, I hope to share with you the wisdom of Confucius as it relates to parenting. I will present Confucius' three universal virtues as the means to develop both your relationship with your children and your relationship with *yourself*. Contained in the three universal virtues are timeless insights; insights that will complement the Western parenting tips and methods you may also be learning. Both the virtues and the parenting skills are vital to help us understand how to best respond to all the complex situations that arise in raising children in the modern world.

Most of the Confucius' teachings in this book are from *Analects*, a book which was written by the students of Confucius. *Analects*, together with *Mencius*, *The Great Learning*, and *Doctrine of the Mean*, are named the "Four Books" of the Confucian Classics.

INTRODUCTION

❧ The Way of the Virtuous Parent ❧

Two thousand five hundred years ago, a Chinese sage named Confucius taught that all the legislation, political promises, social programs, and religious revivals would amount to nothing without the presence of one thing: Virtue. He viewed virtue (*Te*) as the most powerful force in the universe—a force that could change all of mankind, one person at a time.

Confucius lived in an age of historical transition and cultural crisis (551–479 B.C.) in the ancient state of Lu. He was born into an era of escalating violence as seven of the most powerful states in the proto-Chinese world warred for supremacy. In a way, there is a certain similarity between his time and ours. He was witnessing a world that was sinking into violence and disorder, a world that was too involved in power struggles and personal gains. *He saw a world where people had failed to see and feel for the importance of virtues in human relationships, a force that could change the way we act toward others, and the way others act toward us.*

Confucius believed that any change we wished to make in our lives must begin *within* ourselves. He called this "cultivation of the mind," which we can understand as the ability to look within ourselves and observe and become aware of our own feelings, thoughts, and behaviors. True cultivation of mind,

Confucius taught, can only be accomplished by embracing virtue. Once virtue was embodied within the soul and became a way of being, an individual could then transform their families, communities, nation, and even the world.

This was as challenging a concept to grasp then as it is now. When Confucius' students did not understand how one individual could have such a great impact upon the world, Confucius told them that this was one of the great secrets of the ancients.

> *Taking his staff, he drew circles within circles in the sand as he taught this lesson:*

> *"When the ancients wished to illustrate virtue through-out the kingdom, they first ordered their own states,*
> *Wishing to order well their states, they first regulated their families.*
> *Wishing to regulate their families, they first cultivated their selves.*
> *Wishing to cultivate their selves, they first changed their hearts.*
> *Wishing to change their hearts, they first sought to be sincere in thought.*
> *Wishing to be sincere in their thoughts, they first sought true knowledge within the soul."*

> *Gazing at the circles, the light of understanding began to shine from the eyes of the students. Yet before they could ask another question, the Master continued:*

> *"Having sought out true knowledge in the soul, they became sincere in their thoughts.*

Their thoughts sincere, their hearts were changed.
Their hearts changed, their selves were transformed.
Their selves transformed, their families were well
* regulated*
Their families well regulated, their states were well
* governed.*
Their states well governed, the kingdom was at peace."
                                        —The Way of Virtue

When we think about and meditate upon Confucius' words, we can begin to understand how virtuous living, like a pebble tossed in a pond, can ripple across all of life. If we cultivate virtue in ourselves, we will affect not only our own lives, but also the lives of all of those around us—expecially our children. It is from this recognition that we will explore the three universal virtues of Confucius' teachings.

❧ VIRTUES AND PARENTING ❧

How do we use virtues to cultivate ourselves from within? Virtue is not the same as moral principles or a code of ethics, which require us to be judged by a certain fixed standard. Virtue is moral character that we cultivate *within* ourselves and that determines the goodness of our own actions. In essence, virtue is about taking the right action for the right result. *The cultivation of virtues will help us gain the insights to make the right choices and perform the right actions.* Confucius believed that virtues show in the excellence of our actions in relationship with other people. How we act toward others affects people in positive or negative ways. When we act with virtue we will always positively affect our relationships as well as our own personal lives.

The power of virtue is in its *influence*. Virtue can gradually change our own behavior, and then through our positive influence, the behavior of the people around us without the use of coercion or violence. It is clear to see how this directly relates to parenting and how it may help us with many of our dilemmas. Parenting in today's world is not easy. There are more parenting books than ever before and yet there also seem to be more problems with today's children. We receive mixed messages every day about what we should consider to be important, or even true, and we can easily lose the focus of what will provide the essential foundation for all our parenting decisions. Virtue can help to remind us of the goodness we must always strive for in ourselves and in our parenting.

Practicing virtue in parenting leads to two distinct benefits. First, it brings about changes within yourself—not just so you are a better parent, but also a better person. Check with your spouse, friends, neighbors and even your dog, they will all be drawn closer to you when you become a bigger person in your heart. Second, it brings about the spontaneous cultivation of virtue in your children. For all parenting experts agree that the most important role model for your child is *you*.

❦ VIRTUE IS THE ROOT ❦

Exemplary persons concentrate their efforts on the root,
for the root having taken hold; the way will grow there from.
(Analects 1.2)

According to Confucius, everything has its roots and its branches. Confucius puts great emphasis on the roots, for the roots come first. The branches, which only grow once the roots have been established, are much less stressed in Confucius' teaching. The order of this sequence cannot be altered. At times, people may fail to distinguish the root from the branches, and so they fail to distinguish between that which should be greatly emphasized and that which should receive less of our attention.

The root of parenting is the rectification of the heart. This will help us withstand difficulties and crises in parenting. A heart that is rectified with virtue will prepare you for all the challenges and the joys in parenting. As we work our way through this book, we will often pause to reflect upon the root and branches of common parenting issues—for only when we find the root will we be able to find the proper solution for each problem.

There is a Chinese saying "Once you get into the habit of doing something, it will become a natural part of you." The cultivation of virtue is not a quick process. There is no button to push for instant download. Virtues can only be learned, experienced, and practiced, and the key is practice, practice, and practice. Eventually you will see that not only will your child start to feel at ease with you, but you will also feel the ease and peace inside yourself.

PART ONE

The Three Universal Virtues

*A person of benevolence is never anxious; a person of wisdom
is never confused; a person of courage is never fearful.*
(Analects 9.29)

Confucius named benevolence, wisdom, and courage the three
universal virtues. They are universally binding and are each
closely related. *Wisdom aims at the knowledge of benevolence,
and courage at its practice.* By learning and practicing these
three virtues, parenting will become simpler because you will
no longer be fundamentally anxious, confused, or fearful.

Does this mean that parents who are anxious, confused, or
fearful in parenting are instantly benevolent, wise, and courageous? The answer is no. A parent who does not care about the
well-being of a child will never be anxious; a parent who does
not bother to learn about the different ways to parent will
never be confused; a parent who is not concerned with the
consequence of his actions will never be fearful. Yet, this does
not mean these parents are virtuous. Only by instilling the
virtues of benevolence, wisdom, and courage will you be able

to see how right decisions will lead to right results, and in so doing you will become free from anxiety, confusion, and fear.

By learning how to apply the three universal virtues in parenting, you will be one big step closer to effective parenting. By incorporating the three virtues in your parental choices (or in any other life choices), you can rest assured that you will be making the right decision. It may not seem as easy as reacting thoughtlessly to a situation in any way you like, but you'll see the difference is in the results you get. *The key is to make the right decision for the right result.* And that is what virtuous parenting is all about.

If you are not familiar with the three virtues of benevolence, wisdom, and courage, it may take a little while for you to get used to applying them to your everyday parental choices. However, once you get to know and appreciate them, you will get into the pattern of asking three simple questions before making any parental decisions: *Is this benevolent? Is this wise? Do I have the courage to pursue the right result?*

In the next three chapters you will learn more about Confucius' three universal virtues and how they can help with your difficult challenges in parenting. By being able to apply them whenever you are at a crossroad, parenting will become more simple and effective, and you will truly become free from anxiety, confusion, and fear.

Chapter One

Benevolence for Reaching the Heart of Your Child

ACCORDING TO CONFUCIUS, BENEVOLENCE IS THE MOST important virtue. The Chinese character for benevolence is made up of two elements, *ren* (person) and *er* (two). In other words, benevolence is relationship oriented, relating one human being to another.

In its simplest form, benevolence can be expressed as "Love your fellow man." Confucius believed that all humans were born with benevolence but that this virtue will wither without cultivation. It is not a ready-made gift, but an accomplishment that one has to achieve. To be benevolent is not what we are as a person, but what we *do* and *become*. Those who uncover the power of benevolence will gradually think and act in a different, more virtuous manner, and eventually will become an exemplary person who will enjoy life even when the world around them—with or without children screaming—is in turmoil. A person of benevolence will not be changed by the environment, but instead will change the environment for the better.

Many people think that cultivating benevolence is to make the lives of others better or to make the world a better place. These are both true, but this overlooks the fact that by practicing benevolence, we are ourselves the beneficiary as well as the benefactor. Benevolence provides us with a more loving way to look at life, a better way to treat the people around us, and a wonderful way to be loved by others.

Benevolence is the force behind a calm and tranquil life, even if you are an over-scheduled mom or dad. Confucius said, *"Those who are benevolent will have nothing to worry or fear."* When asked if that means that those who have no worries or fears can necessarily claim themselves to be benevolent, Confucius answered, *"If examining oneself and you have nothing to regret, why be worried or fearful?"* (Analects 9.29)

❖ BENEVOLENCE AND PARENTING ❖

Confucius believed that benevolence has different meanings for different people. For a student who was impulsive and violent, benevolence meant patience and kindness. For a student who was shy and timid, benevolence meant the ability to be strong when it came to fighting for what is right. In parenting, benevolence will also mean different things at different times and will express itself in different ways according to your nature. If you are permissive, you may see benevolence as firmness and strength, while if you are authoritative, you will see it as patience and understanding.

The Five Merits of the Benevolent Parent
Though everyone's definition of benevolence may be a little different, the following five merits of benevolent individuals

hold true for all. When asked about the merits of benevolence, Confucius listed these five:

> *They are respectfulness, forgiveness, trustworthiness,*
>   *diligence, and generosity.*
> *If you are respectful, you will not suffer humiliation*
> *If you are forgiving, you win the support of many*
> *If you are trustworthy, others will trust and rely on you*
> *If you are diligent, you will be successful*
> *If you are generous, you be able to employ others effectively.*
> (Analects 17.6)

We can all apply this to our parenting styles to see that:

- If we respect our children, which is not the same as indulging them, we will not induce contempt from them.
- If we forgive and understand, while teaching them the lesson behind their mistakes, we will win our children's hearts.
- If we can prove ourselves to be trustworthy, our children will trust and rely on our guidance.
- If we are diligent and practice good parenting, we will become successful parents.
- If we are generous with our time, care, and love we will gain our children's heartfelt dedication.

For many people, the five merits of benevolence all sound so familiar. Most people are respectful to their boss, forgiving to their spouse, trustworthy to their friends, diligent in their work, and generous to the needy. *But the five merits of benevolence may have been neglected in relationship to their children.* Often people do not realize the power of these five merits in the arena of parenting. They do not realize that their children's behavior, both good and bad, is directly related to their own actions. In other words, children are, in fact, reacting to their parents' actions every day.

❧ ACTIONS OF A BENEVOLENT PARENT ❧

Examine Yourself before You Blame Others
Benevolent persons make demands on themselves;
petty persons make demands on others. (Analects 15.21)

It is almost impossible for even the best parents to go through parenthood without encountering some kind of problem in their parenting. When trouble occurs, it is important to review and examine one's own behavior first before blaming others. It is common to hear people blaming children's problems on the media or the values of popular culture, on their peer groups, schools, and often, on the children themselves. Benevolence asks for self-examination.

The reward for self-examination is threefold. First of all, we will be able to see our own mistakes that might have been overlooked. Secondly, we will be able to learn from those mistakes and avoid making them again. Thirdly, by being able to admit our own mistakes, we will be able to be more patient, because only those who admit their own mistakes will truly understand how difficult it is to correct them and change.

For example, if your child has lied to you, do not immediately blame him or her for their dishonesty. Instead, reflect on what you could have done to prevent the misbehavior. Benevolent parents will question themselves as well as their children in their search for answers. Did we appear to be too stubborn and uncompromising to our child? Are we really too stubborn and uncompromising? If the answer is yes, we can learn our mistake and further investigate the root of the problem.

Children, especially young children, do not lie for fun. They lie because they are afraid to tell the truth. Some parents think that fear will contribute to their children's obedience, but fear often trains them to achieve their goals by lying or doing things behind your back. This is too big a price to pay. Be firm with what is not acceptable, but try to be reasonable and teach your children to achieve their goals by communicating with you and not by lying to you.

Admitting our own mistakes is difficult for our egos, but it is only by graciously admitting our own flaws to ourselves that we get to understand why our children cannot be flawless. For example, only if we admit to ourselves that we are procrastinating at work can we truly understand why it is so difficult for our children to stop procrastinating when it comes to doing their schoolwork.

Mistakes May Be Blessings in Disguise
When benevolent persons make mistakes,
they do not hesitate to reform. (Analects 1.8)

Benevolence first opens us up to self-examination, as we discussed above. However, once we have reviewed and examined our own behavior, we must be ready to acknowledge our own mistakes, if any, and reform. Let's take a common example. Imagine that your three-year-old son has just burned his hand on the stove in the kitchen. You might have told him a hundred times that the kitchen is definitely a no-entry zone for him, but he is only a curious and careless child. A benevolent person will admit their own carelessness and instead of just shouting at the child for his disobedience, will start thinking about installing a safety gate to prevent the child from going into the kitchen when someone is cooking. Looking for ways to remedy the problem ourselves, and admitting any mistakes we may have made, are the first steps towards finding out what needs to be done to avoid repeating the same mistake again. Think of it this way, if you do not admit your own carelessness when your child burns his hand and install a safety gate, the next time he might end up with a pot of boiling hot water on his face.

Always Act with Sincere Intentions

Benevolence involves being the first to willingly take on a difficult task and the last to think about reward or recognition. (Analects 6.22)

Parenting is no easy task, and it seems to be getting harder and harder in today's world. Benevolence helps us accept the challenge willingly for the sake of our children and not the sake of reward or recognition for ourselves. You will have more patience and kindness when your intention is sincere. When you focus on the well-being of your child, and not on reward or recognition for yourself, you will find it easier to differentiate the right responses from the wrong ones.

In parenting, having the right goal is in fact the best guideline to help you make the right parenting decisions. When our goal is clear and full of good intention for the well-being of our child, our energy will focus on doing just that. On the other hand, when our goal is self-serving rewards or recognition, our actions will also follow accordingly. For example, if your goal is to experience power and to feel the thrill of being able to control others, then don't give your children any opportunity or support to learn to make their own decisions. But don't be surprised if your children end up resentful, spiteful, and unable to function independently in the world. Or if you want to be affirmed by being recognized as "the Most Easygoing Dad in the Neighborhood" by your daughter and her friends, then by all means indulge her every whim but don't be surprised if, from an excess of freedom and a lack of healthy boundaries, she grows up to be manipulative, selfish, spoiled, and even harms herself by not having a healthy sense of safe and moral parameters.

Benevolence requires that one work hard for the right result. It is so much easier to buy your three-year-old the candy bar he wants in the supermarket then to have to learn how to deal with his screams and unreasonable demands in front of all the people around you. It is not easy to let your preteen daughter go to her first summer camp hundreds of miles away from home when it feels so much "safer" to have her attend summer school in your own neighborhood. It always *seems* harder to put the wellness of others before our own, but if we parent with benevolence, we will receive a different kind of reward and recognition from our children, which may prove to be far more deeply fulfilling than we ever could have imagined.

Practice Self-Control
Benevolence is to restrain oneself from what you want to say and do, so that one can retain propriety. (Analects 12.1)

Benevolence helps parents to engage in self-control and maintain the standard of socially acceptable conduct or speech. This is much easier when we are dealing with our friends. When it comes to our own children we tend to take more liberties with propriety. Imagine yourself shouting and yelling at your friends when they do something wrong. If you did that, it might be a while before you hear from them again. Imagine shouting and yelling at your child for something not acceptable to you. Your child may fear and obey you, but do you know what will he be thinking? Does he really understand the lesson or is he just being obedient?

When we practice self-control—when we allow ourselves a moment to pause and see the situation carefully—we will think twice about what we want to say or do. When we are upset or angry, we often say and do things we wish, in retrospect, that we hadn't. Do not underestimate the effect of abusing words; they could hurt a child as badly as your fist. In fact, bruises and wounds heal in time, but pain caused by abusing words from parents might last a lifetime. The virtue of benevolence teaches us to control our impulsiveness, to not say and do things that are inappropriate. Many parenting experts suggest a time-out—a cool down period—for both parents and children when tempers are roused. You will be surprised at how much more easily you can control yourself if you take a five-minute time-out when you want to hurt your child with words or action. Not only will your child respect you more, but you will also be able to see your child as a young and immature person who also deserves to be guided with respect.

❧ Benevolent Behavior ❧
for Effective Parenting

Be Firm, Determined, Honest, and Deliberate
Being firm, determined, honest, and deliberate in speech is close to benevolent conduct. (Analects 13.27)

Effective parenting brings results. Benevolent conduct helps us to accomplish what we want to achieve. If we want to be an effective parent, practicing benevolent conduct is a good way to start.

Be firm with discipline. When it comes to discipline, you need to be firm with what you believe is important to raise a happy, healthy, and well-balanced child. Do not give in to the pitiful look of your beloved little angel when she needs to be disciplined so she can learn right from wrong; likewise, don't allow yourself to become intimidated by the angry look on your teenager's face when you set healthy boundaries on their freedom. Being firm does not necessarily take shouting and yelling. *Parents can be firm by being gentle and soft-spoken.* All you want to do is to let your child know that you are firm because it is your responsibility to discipline him well. However, it is important to make sure that you are firm *and* reasonable.

Be determined to be the best parent possible. Where there is a will, there is a way. If you are determined to be the best parent to your child, there is really nothing that can stop you from achieving that goal. If you lack the knowledge, learn from others and from all the parenting help available. If you lack the perfect personality, cultivate what it takes to be the kind of parent you want yourself to be. Once you set your mind to become "the best" parent for your child, all paths will lead you there.

Be honest with yourself. In parenting, it is as important to be honest with yourself as it is to be honest with your children. You need to be honest with your children so that you can gain their trust. Honesty requires you to go deeper into your subconscious mind, to see that you are not lying to yourself. You need to be honest with yourself so that you can gain insight into what is genuinely going on in front of you and within you. What you like to believe is going on might not be what is really going on.

Be careful with what you say to your child. Confucius taught about the importance of speech in human relationships. Confucius said, *"A benevolent person is slow and careful in speech."* (Analects 12.3) So think carefully before you speak, especially when you are angry or discouraged. Sometimes if you don't know what to say, be silent. Silence might not help to solve any problem, but at least it will not cause more harm or any immediate damage.

Accept Each Other's Differences
A benevolent person seeks harmony and not sameness.
(Analects 13.23)

You might not like your daughter's pink highlights or purple hair; you might not be able to stand your son's low cut oversized pants, or you may not understand why your daughter's jeans need to look like they are one size too small, but that doesn't mean that what you dislike is definitely wrong. Your child might not think that all you do is right either.

In order to seek harmony in your parent/child relationship, you and your child will both need to accept each other's differences. Acceptance is not the same as approval. There are things you need to accept even if you don't approve of them, but always set healthy boundaries so your son or daughter can get the guidance and foundation they need for an ethical, moral life. You might not approve of your child's choice of major in college, but you will have to accept her and her decision. This will also be a very good lesson for your child to learn. Your child might not approve of your extravagant or stingy life style, but he will have to learn how to accept you for who you are. Benevolence seeks harmony and not sameness. From the head of a nation to the head of a family, this is one important principle to model so children and young people can learn how to build a more peaceful world.

Love . . . and Express Your Love in All Possible Ways
To be benevolent is to love the other person. (Analects 12.22)

Benevolence, in its simplest form, is loving another person. But it is not as simple as it sounds. Most parents will not doubt for a moment that they love their children. They take care of their children, provide them with the best life has to offer, devote their time and energy to raising them well. Every parent makes some kind of sacrifice for his or her children. But what happens when the child defies or rebels? Can you still say, "I love you" to a child who screams, "I hate you?"

Benevolence requires us to love others even when we are disappointed or angry with them. We will discuss how benevolence can help us control our anger in the next section, but for now, let us concentrate on how we could still love a child who has broken our heart. The key is how to *see* the child in a benevolent way. It is easy to love a sweet baby who is cute and affectionate. But what happens when your child is doing everything you hate. He may be rude, defiant, and so different from the younger child you loved so much. Do you only hate what he did, or are you starting to hate him? It is a scary thought, but it is something we will have to deal with before we can truly understand what benevolence is all about.

Many parenting experts have advised parents to separate a child's actions from the child. I found this the most difficult part of parenting, and it took me a long time to discover that the only way we can be benevolent even when we are really angry with our children is to put on our "Benevolent Glasses." Through this pair of glasses, you will see your child as he or she *really* is . . . a two-and-one-half-year-old who hates you because he hates the way you boss him around but still loves everything else about you; a twelve-year-old who acts like twenty-one because she is scared, confused, and thinks that you won't allow her to find her own identity. Only by seeing with benevolence can we act with benevolence, and only by acting with benevolence can we truly raise a child who will be happy and successful in life.

In understanding our love for another, we need to, again, look into our intention. Confucius stressed "Sincerity of Intention." Do we love our son only if he is hardworking? Do we love our daughter only if she is obedient? Or do we love our children unconditionally? This brings us back to our previous discussion on the goal of self-serving rewards and recognition versus care for our child's long-term well-being.

If there is one thing that we absolutely cannot do without in successful parenting, it is *unconditional love*. A child will need to know that you love him even if he has done something bad. It is dangerous to even suggest to a child that you will take your love away if he does something wrong. *A child needs to know that you will love him no matter what happens.* Your love for your child should not fade even if he has committed the worst crime on earth. You definitely do not approve of his wrongdoing, but that does not mean you should love him less.

His friends, his lover, or his spouse may stop loving him, but never his mother and father.

A child who thinks his parents do not love him can never learn how to love himself, and loving ourselves is the foundation for a happy and well-balanced person. As long as children know that their parents love them unconditionally, they will return the love in one way or another. This leads us to another important point . . . do your children feel that you love them?

Show and Express Your Love in Every Way Possible

No human can resist the genuine love of another human being, whether that person is a parent, a lover, a friend, a neighbor, or even someone he once considered an enemy. In the same way, if there ever comes a time that you doubt your love for your child who has broken your heart, remember that he or she was the same loving child who once whispered in your ears "I love you, mommy" or "I love you, daddy." Give him or her a chance to say it again.

❦ BENEVOLENCE FOR CONTROLLING ANGER ❦

Though benevolence will inspire us to act with love and respect, we may still feel like there is one factor that keeps us from "doing it right." That is the *anger* factor. For people like me who entered parenthood with "short fused" stamped on their forehead and "devoted parent" imprinted on their heart, parenting is bound to be an uphill race. Anger and parental devotion just do not mix; one of them will have to go if you want to save yourself from the pain and agony in parenting. My decision was to keep the devotion and try to conquer anger.

Two Opposing Forces

Benevolence inspires us to love and be kind to another person. Anger makes us want to do just the opposite. It makes us want to hurt the other person because the other person has caused us pain.

To manage anger with benevolence is to learn how to eliminate the desire to hurt another person. We can do this by cultivating benevolence in our heart. The calmness will then come from within and not just from diverting our focus to things outside of us, like music or a cool drink. The focus will need to be on our *benevolent thoughts* which will help us to find a way to love the other person who has irritated us. In confronting our children and their disobedience, benevolence will prompt us to understand and help them; instead of doing all we can to hurt them with words or actions. Consider this example.

> *Karen was the mother of an eleven-year-old boy, Charles. She had always wanted to give her best to her child and to become an excellent parent. She studied parenting books, attended parenting classes, consulted parenting experts and even went out of her way to learn yoga so that she could slow down and be more relaxed with life. She followed everything that she studied to the best she could and was happy to see that she was making good progress.*
>
> *When Karen told Charles that she had programmed the computer to restrict and monitor his Internet use at home, Charles slammed the door in her face. When Karen demanded that he come out and apologize, he shouted, "get lost" from the other side of the door. This was totally unexpected, and Karen*

found herself holding her breath outside Charles's room, with enough dynamite to blow the door open.

For a second, Karen thought she could handle this. She had learned from her parenting books about how to handle such a situation. She remembered exactly what some of her parenting books had taught her to do—take a time-out, go for a walk, take a shower, listen to some soft music, practice slow and deep breathing, stay calm, don't reward your children's misbehavior with your anger, think of a time you had good control, let your anger out slowly by talking with your child. . . . All these things seemed to have helped in the past but Karen's hands were still shaking and her heart started beating faster and faster.

In the intensity of her anger, Karen started to think that maybe shouting back at her son might soothe things a bit for her, but all the books said that she should not react to her child's bad mouthing. All the books said it was nothing personal, that the child just did not like what she had done, not who she was. But still, Karen could not stop playing and replaying the terrible scene in her mind. Maybe she should just "get lost," take the easy way out, and let Charles ruin his life with all the evil temptations on the Internet. Karen felt her anger surging inside her until she finally said to herself, "Enough is enough. I am who I am." It is so much easier to react to her anger and just do what feels good in that moment.

No matter how much Karen loved her son, it was a great challenge for her to keep cool under these circumstances. Telling herself that she loved her son was not enough for her when

Charles slammed the door in her face. Having a child slam the door in your face and shout, "get lost," is *definitely* not acceptable, and under no circumstance should a parent allow such rudeness. Yet, Karen needed to be patient and tolerant, not only with her son's misbehavior, but with her own thoughts and action.

Anger was telling Karen to hurt her son. But if hurting a child verbally or physically were effective in correcting bad behaviors, then abused children would be the most well behaved children of all. This is obviously not the case. Shouting and hitting will only bring about fear or rebellion in a child. The child might behave properly only because he or she is scared. Ruling by fear only works as long as the child is still afraid of you and the punishment, and as long as you are in your commander-in-chief uniform. Can you imagine what will happen when your child no longer fears you and your punishment, or that commander-in-chief is not around to watch over him? In addition, the damage done to a child in exchange for such obedience is enormous and irreversible.

Karen was left with three choices: She could react to her anger and hurt her son to make herself feel better. She could turn away as if nothing had happened and concentrate on her busy social life. Or she could practice the Three Steps of Anger Management with Benevolence (that we'll discuss next) to calm herself down and get the best result.

The Three Steps of Anger Management with Benevolence

Step One
Cool off with Benevolent Thoughts

Benevolent thoughts in relationship to anger are like water to fire. The bigger the fire, the more water we need to put it out. The angrier we are, the more benevolent thoughts we need to calm us down. Yet having water and aiming incorrectly does not help put out the fire either. That is why we need precision, which can only be achieved with a clear mind. This is when we need to have a timeout. We need a timeout to clear our mind of the smoke and to see clearly what is happening so that then we can see how benevolence thoughts can help. There are four benevolent thoughts that can help and they are as follows.

1. Understand the Other Person.

> *Do not fret when the other person*
> *does not understanding you; Fret when*
> *you do not understand the other person.*
> (Analects 1.16)

You must try to understand why the person made you angry. In Karen's case, Karen will need to understand why her child misbehaved and find a reason to be angry at the behavior and not the child. It is only by asking "Why" *from the child's point of view* that we will understand why he acted the way he did.

In a previous example, Charles was rude to his mother because he was angry with her for controlling and monitoring his Internet use. He was also angry with her because he felt she had decided to take away, or at least reduce, his joy of life without even telling him about it. On top of that, he felt that she did not show any respect for his privacy by installing a monitor program in his computer without telling him anything about it in advance. Once Karen starts to understand the way that her son is thinking, her heart will feel less disturbed.

Can we do this in all situations? Yes. Even if we do not completely comprehend our children's point of view, taking a practical look at the situation will help us understand our children a little bit more. Close your eyes and see your children as the individuals they are becoming and realize that they are not there yet. Depending on the age of the child, we should take into account that their immaturity is one great factor that drove them to do the "bad" things they did. A little understanding will go a long way.

2. Have Compassion.

If successful in extracting the truth of a criminal case, do not congratulate yourself, but have compassion for them.
(Analects 19.19)

A benevolent person needs to have compassion for the person who misbehaves. Karen's son could have explained nicely to his mother why he was so upset with the new set up, but he was only eleven years old and immature in his judgment. Instead of condemning your child right away, try to feel for him—you will certainly feel better inside if you do.

This takes more than just understanding his side of the story—it asks you to feel his pain or other emotions. Karen's son was very angry when he slammed the door. If Charles were a benevolent young man, he would have felt the pain in his mother's heart when he shouted "get lost." Compassion is feeling another's

emotions, and it is the most crucial response to cultivate to prevent violence against another human being
or against any other living being on earth. Do you ever
feel the pain of another person? The more you can *feel*
your child's fear and pain when you hurt him with
your hand or your words, the harder it is for you to
assault him. In addition, the more your child learns
about benevolence, the more he will appreciate the
effects of his actions on his parents and others.

3. Look at Your Own Contribution to the Problem
*I have yet to meet the person who could perceive his
own mistake and inwardly criticize himself.*
(Analects 5.27)

Confucius regrets that he could not find people who
are able to criticize themselves. What could Karen
have done to avoid her son's outburst? She could have
discussed the new Internet setup with her son before
installing it, she could have taught him about anger
management, or she could have taught him the
importance of respect in the house. Only when we
look at our own contribution to a situation will we see
it fairly and honestly. If you did something wrong,
admit it. Just admitting it to yourself is a great help. Not
only will your admittance help to resolve the situation,
but you will also be teaching your child an important
lesson on self-reflection and accepting responsibility.

4. Kindness is Irresistible
Do not impose on others what you do not desire.
(Analects 12.2)

In other words, don't do to others what you do not want others to do to you. This is one principle that we have heard over and over again in different texts and different languages. It is the golden rule of benevolence. If each one of us can say this quote in our minds each time we think of hurting another person, physically or verbally, a lot of unkind acts can been avoided. Everybody loves to be treated kindly—even the most unkind person in the world will not be able to resist kindness.

Karen could kick open the door, or unlock it with her key, drag Charles out of his room, and act like a raging bull. She could say and do all the things that will serve the purpose of hurting Charles. And do you know what Charles would be thinking? He would be thinking of how to hurt his mother back, for he is also very angry. And the cycle will go on and on.

There is another possibility. Karen could treat Charles with kindness and respect just like she would like to be treated, after all that is what Karen would like to teach Charles. She could sit down with her son after both of them have calmed down and have recuperated from the terrible incident. She should act kindly not because she wants to be permissive but because she knows that the power of kindness will get her the result she desires. If Karen is able to clear her mind of anger and is able to *respond* instead of *react* to her son's rudeness, then it is time to move on to step two and step three.

Step Two
Think Clearly with Wisdom

We need benevolence to help clear our minds when we are angry, but we also need the virtue of wisdom to help us to have the knowledge to think properly. Thinking clearly is important because only when we have a clear mind can we foresee the consequences of our actions *fast*—before we say or do anything. Provided you have been able to instill benevolence and calm yourself (if not, take a longer time-out and go through the benevolent thoughts again) and are no longer angry, keeping quiet and pretending that nothing has happened can be as unwise as saying the wrong thing. Eleven-year old Charles needs some guidance from his mother. He needs to learn how to deal with his anger and he needs to be properly disciplined for his misbehavior.

In chapter 5, we will talk more about how to be an inspiring teacher. But for now, the key is to be able to focus on achieving the right results and seeing the consequences of our own actions. Karen needs to achieve three things. First, she needs to teach Charles about good manners. She needs to let Charles know that door slamming and bad mouthing are absolutely not allowed in their house. (She will also need to remember this herself.) Second, she has to teach Charles to fight for what he believes in by reasoning and not by violence or profanity. Third, she needs to let her son know that she is an understanding mother who wants the best for her son.

Karen needs to hear what Charles has to say, by whatever listening methods she has learned, and then tell Charles her side of the story. It is always better when both parent and child can come to a mutual understanding for then it will not become a power struggle. However, depending on the age of the child and his maturity, parents should still have the final say. But remember, even if the child acts up again during the discussion, make sure you have the wisdom to recognize that you are the adult dealing with a child, and you should be the one who is calm and in control of the situation.

Step Three
Full Speed Ahead with Courage

Courage is necessary to carry out the act of benevolence. Most people think of courage as being brave to do what they *want* to do. In many cases, it is true. It is courageous to climb Mt. Everest or to train for a triathlon. *Yet, in parenting, parents also need to have the courage to restrain from doing what they want to do, especially when they are angry.* When a person is angry, the natural response is "fight or flight." When our children misbehave and antagonize us, it is natural that we want to fight the child and win or to simply deny the problem and run away from it.

Confucius said that courage without the knowledge of benevolence is dangerous. Having the courage to hurt our children when we are angry is indeed very dangerous—to the children and to us. Ever feel your heart pounding and your hands sweating when you scream at your child? That is hazardous to your health. On the other hand, running away from the problem is just as dangerous. You deprive your child of the chance to learn from his mistake and it could be the beginning of a nightmare for both you and your child. Instead of running away from the problem, examine yourself for any mistake you have made. Confucius said, "Knowing your mistake is close to courage." If you do find your own mistake, take more courage and admit it to yourself and your child. Depending on the age and maturity of your child, explain to him that everyone makes mistakes, but the most important point is to learn from the mistakes and improve ourselves.

This will teach your child the importance of self-examination and he will respect you more for your honesty and courage.

The partnership of benevolence, wisdom, and courage will enable you to restrain yourself from your "fight or flight" response, and convert the energy to help you stay strong and resist the temptation. Only after you can stay away from reacting impulsively can you cool yourself down with benevolence, and only when you are calm can you recap all the wisdom you have cultivated and act in a wise and courageous way.

Benevolence is a powerful quality and with it we can deepen the relationships we have with our children and ourselves. We can manage our anger by transforming it into understanding, compassion, and self-awareness. The more virtue you have cultivated inside yourself, the more "water" you will have stored to put out the fire. All the skills you have learned from the parenting books will be more effective when your mind is clear and your heart is full of love.

❧ THE NINE THOUGHTS ❦
OF A BENEVOLENT PERSON

A benevolent person has nine thoughts:
When looking, think if you have seen clearly
When listening, think if you have heard correctly
When communicating, think if you reflect gentleness
When facing others, think if you show respectfulness
When speaking, think if you are sincere and truthful
When at work, think if you are serious with the work
When in doubt, think if you have sought advice from others
When angry, think if you have considered the consequence of this action

> *When a gain is possible, think if your action is appro-*
> *priate and right.* (Analects 16.10)

These nine thoughts are actions that we should take in all of our life experiences. When we apply these nine thoughts to parenting, they look like this:

- When looking at your child, or at his or her problem, think if you have seen clearly.
- When listening to your child, think if you have heard correctly.
- When communicating with your child, think if you present yourself to be kind and gentle.
- When dealing with your child face-to-face, think if you show respect for him as a person.
- When speaking with your child, think if you are honest and sincere with your words.
- When parenting, think if you take the task seriously.
- When in doubt with what to do with your child, think if you will seek help from others.
- When you are angry, think about the consequence of your words or action. Taking five deep breaths before responding might help.
- When you are able to achieve your goal in parenting, think to see if your achievement is for your well-being or for the good of *your child*.

All these nine thoughts are interrelated and work best when all are employed. Reflect upon these goals as you work benevolence into your heart and as you deepen your relationship with your children. Every time we act with one of these thoughts in mind, we are one step closer to being a benevolent parent.

Simple Answers to Frequently Asked Questions

WHAT IS BENEVOLENCE?

Benevolence is the virtue that helps us change the way we see and treat others by feeling others' need for love and kindness. This is the most important virtue for all human relationships because it gives us the power to change ourselves and the people around us. Just like violence, benevolence is contagious and can spread quickly from one human being to another.

WHY DO PARENTS NEED BENEVOLENCE?

Parents need benevolence because it will enable them to truly see and understand their children as they are, the problems as they stand, and their parental goals as they should be. They also need benevolence because it will help them to change themselves from within so that they can become the best parents they can become.

WHEN DO WE MOST NEED BENEVOLENCE?

Benevolence is needed 24/7 in parenting, but it is needed most acutely when things are getting out of control and we are in anger and in doubt of our love for our children. Benevolence will help us restore parental love even when the child standing in front of us no longer seems lovable.

HOW DO WE APPLY BENEVOLENCE TO PARENTING?

Here is an example of how to apply the virtue of benevolence in a challenging situation. You find out that your daughter is using drugs. You are furious and disappointed. It is hard to be conscientious with your response. Benevolence helps us choose between doing more harm to the child and our parent/child relationship *or* looking into the root of the problem and finding the courage to deal with it. Benevolent parents choose to help their beloved child overcome the problem instead of driving the child further away from us. This is when self-control and self-examination need to come together with the nine thoughts and five merits of benevolent parents. Only benevolence can help us choose the right path.

Chapter Two

Wisdom for Making
Wise Parenting Decisions

WISDOM IS THE VIRTUE THAT ALLOWS US TO MAKE GOOD choices and sound decisions. Unlike intelligence, wisdom is not inborn—it needs to be cultivated. It is shaped not only by education but also by thinking and experiencing. The virtue of wisdom is all about having the right knowledge to make the right decisions. You'll find that you'll need different kinds for wisdom for different kinds of decisions in life.

When asked about wisdom, Confucius said, *"Know your fellow men."* (Analects 12.23) In other words, to have wisdom is to have the knowledge of human beings. That is why it is always good to study child psychology when trying to deal with a child's problem. If we do not know the thoughts of our children, it will be hard to predict their actions and behavior. Confucius also said that a man of wisdom never has two minds. This means that a wise person is never in two minds in his judgment of right and wrong. A parent of wisdom will have no doubt about benevolence, making it easy to differentiate a right decision from a wrong decision.

❧ Wisdom and Parenting ❧

Just as in other important areas of our lives, the cultivation of wisdom in parenting takes more than just intelligence. It has to start with acquiring and *perfecting the knowledge*—understanding the root of any given problem or situation. Confucius named perfecting the knowledge as the essential and most fundamental element in regulating a family. This wisdom can also be the most important element to ruling the nation and bringing peace to the world. Confucius identified it like this:

> *Wishing to regulate one's family, you must first*
> cultivate yourself.
> *Wishing to cultivate yourself, you must first* rectify
> your mind.
> *Wishing to rectify your mind, you must first seek to*
> *be* sincere in thought.
> *Wishing to be sincere in thought, you must first seek the*
> perfecting of knowledge. (The Great Learning)

Let's take a closer look at each of these four elements.

1. Perfecting Knowledge: Find the Root of the Problem

Ever since kindergarten, my son had always been a very good student with good grades and no disciplinary problems. However, two months into seventh grade, I received a phone call that woke me up like a super-sized alarm clock. His math teacher called and told me that he did not turn in his homework and did not prepare for his test. She also told me that if my son did this in her class, he was probably doing it in other classes, too. She was right. Two more teachers called the next day, telling me the same thing about my son. When I asked my son about it, his reply was even more alarming, he said, "I'm not that bad, you should see Jason, he doesn't do any homework and he fights all the time in school. At least I stay out of the fights."

My perfect little boy who was a recipient of the President Award just two years earlier had suddenly turn into Jason II? This is when I knew I was in trouble and needed to do something about it. I knew I would have to find out the whole truth behind what had happened. I would have to work at perfecting the knowledge—which would allow me to find the root of the problem, foresee what this problem will lead to, and help me to decide what to do.

A few things came to my mind: the bad influence of his friend, the possibility that his schoolwork may be getting too difficult, or that it may be just a stage. But I realized that these were all only branches of the problem. I needed to investigate and find the root of the problem that had caused him to change so drastically.

After much thought and research into the possible roots of this problem, I finally saw the light: the root of the problem was his overly controlling mother. His "new" behavior was a warning sign that he wanted to fight for some control of his life. My controlling parenting style had caused him to move away from me and to experiment with a new lifestyle that he chose. His new friend and his new study habits were his way of telling me that he wanted a taste of independence.

I consider preteen and early teen years to be the most vulnerable years for children because they are too young to know the proper way to fight for independence. Children often feel helpless and at times angry at parental control. Many girls develop eating disorders and others start to engage in substance abuse and sexual activities because they know that no matter how authoritative and controlling a parent can be, they will always have the final say over what they want to do to their own bodies. My investigation had led me to believe that my son's drawback in school was actually a blessing in disguise for me. Things could have been much worse.

To make the investigation more complete, I also needed to foresee what was to come. It was not hard to predict the results of his behavior: Failure in school, disciplinary problems, a rotten parent/child relationship . . . I knew I had to do something about it, fast. The incident was a wake up call for me to investigate and perfect my knowledge as a parent. I consider myself lucky to have been able to respond to these signals in time to make things better before it was too late. *As parents, we have to watch out for signs of problems before the time bomb blows up.* We often fail to be aware of the problems right in front of our eyes because we fail to see what we don't like to see.

The virtue of wisdom teaches us to always be aware of what is happening around us. A wise parent does not just sit around reading parenting books. It really does not matter how wise we are if we are not aware of what is happening in the life of our children. This is easier when children are young. Once they approach adolescence, the key word is communication, for even the wisest parent will not be able to do a good job if his children are blocking him out.

After we investigate the problem and perfect the knowledge, it is time to ask ourselves what we are going to do about it, and what is the right thing to do.

2. Sincere in Thought—Prevent Self-Deception

Like any other parent, my new discovery about the root of my son's problems was hard to accept. There must be something else or someone else that was guilty and should stand trial with me. But after thinking about it over and over again, I had decided that I should have the courage to be honest and accept what I had discovered about myself.

It is never easy to admit, even to yourself, that what you thought was well-intentioned parenting had turned out to be harmful to your child. The feelings of guilt, fear, confusion, and even anger can easily make us turn away from facing the truth. However, it can also be an opportunity for us to see ourselves like never before. It is only when we admit a mistake that we can try to change ourselves and correct the wrong. Confucius said, *"Not correcting a mistake is a mistake."* (Analects 15.30)

To make the decision to change is comparatively easy; to change is not. Confucius said that all changes would have to come from within; people today also think likewise. Karim Hajee, founder of the Creating Power System, wrote in his book *Creating Power: The Secrets to Success and Happiness* that "your subconscious mind does not know right from wrong . . . your subconscious mind or your spirit simply acts on the instructions received from your conscious mind. Those *instructions* are your *thoughts*. Thoughts repeated over and over again become *beliefs*. Beliefs are planted on your subconscious mind and they become your reality. Everything begins with your thoughts, which are in your conscious mind. In order to change your reality you need to change your beliefs. In order to change your beliefs you need to change your thoughts."

If you want to be healthy and strong and believe that you could stay fit and healthy, your subconscious mind will drive you to wake up early, exercise before you go to work, study about nutrition, cut down on alcohol and your favorite ice cream, take up yoga, and so on. However, if you believe that you have bad genes and are meant to be the weak and unhealthy, you will allow yourself to indulge in unhealthy food and become a couch potato. The same will go for your study, your career, your marriage and then, of course, parenting. If you believe that you want be a kind and gentle or virtuous parent, you will become a kind and understanding or virtuous parent. If you believe that you need to be controlling and criticizing to raise your child well, you will become controlling and criticizing. *The only way you can genuinely change yourself is when the virtue of wisdom enlightens you with what is right and what is wrong to do.* That is why it is very important for you to understand and believe in what is right for you, so that the power of your subconscious mind will help you get there.

This is why wisdom is so important. Without wisdom, we will not know what is right and what is wrong, and when we cannot tell right from wrong, we might actually program our mind with wrong thinking. The wrong thinking will then lead us to our wrong action, which in turn will bring about the wrong result. In the *Doctrine of the Mean*, Confucius said, *"If a man does not understand what is good, he will not attain sincerity in himself."* That is why the feeling for right and wrong is said to be the beginning of wisdom.

3. Rectify the Mind—Avoid Wrong Judgment Caused by Your Emotions

Was I angry with my son? Was I afraid that he might get worse in school and be involved in more dangerous problems in his adolescence? Was I upset that he had disappointed me? Was I distressed by the situation? The answer to all the above questions was "yes." Did I have the clarity in my mind to do what is right? The answer was "no," or at least not right away. We are human, and emotions are part of our being. Our minds can't make wise decisions if they are under the influence of emotions such as passion, anger, terror, sorrow, distress, or even when we are carried away with joy.

To be a wise parent, we must first rectify our minds so that we can be clear of the clouding influence of strong emotions before we make any judgment or decisions. If we are able to see with clarity, not only will we be able to access the wisdom inside us, but we will also be able to be fair and justified regardless of whether or not we have a good day.

4. Cultivation of the Person— Enlightened with Wisdom

It was after I sought to "perfect the knowledge" that I discovered the root of the problem. It was after I became sincere in thought that I was brave enough to be honest with myself about the truth. It was after I was able to rectify my mind that I got to see my son without the distorting influence of my anger and disappointment, and to feel my love for him even if he did get off track. It was only when I knew how to avoid unwise decisions that I could cultivate those qualities in myself that would make me become the parent who truly could help my son.

I did not solve the problem because I was a wise parent; it was just the other way around. The problem had given me the opportunity to cultivate myself and I became wiser in the process. When we better ourselves in this way, we are bringing ourselves to a higher state of awareness. Once we reach this awareness we can prevent ourselves from acting incorrectly in the same way in the future.

In his book *Wisdom of Ages* Wayne Dyer says that "enlightenment is not an attainment, it is a realization. Once you reach this realization, everything appears to have changed; yet no change has taken place. It is as if you had been going through life with your eyes closed and then suddenly opened them. Now you can see, but the world hasn't changed; you simply see it with new eyes." This is so true for the cultivation of good parenting. When you cultivate the virtue of wisdom, you will be able to see your children in a new perspective that your passion or your anger had kept you from seeing before. You will also see things far beyond tomorrow that will alert you to act accordingly. Once you are able to obtain the clarity in your mind to make the best choice for you and your child, you will understand what Confucius meant by "Those with wisdom will not be confused."

❧ THE WISDOM TO MAKE GOOD DECISIONS ❧

We might need intelligence for rocket science, but wisdom is what we need to make right choices in everyday life. Even for those with a superior IQ or a Ph. D., when it comes to parenting, intelligence does not guarantee wisdom. Unless you were taught how to make good decisions on your own when you were young, you will probably still be learning these skills as an adult. Age and experience do help, but the bottom line is whether or not you have the knowledge to foresee the consequences of your decisions.

Wise decision-making is very important in raising our children—not only in making our own parenting decisions, but also in helping our children make decisions of their own. Unfortunately, there is no set rule for parents to follow regarding when children should be allowed to make decisions. It all depends on the maturity of the child and what kind of decisions needs to be made. The question is more on *what* then *when*. Parents should use their wisdom to decide what kind of decisions their own children are capable of making at different ages. For example, how should you respond if your child wants to give up his college scholarship because he wants to start a family with his high school sweetheart right after graduation? This is a big decision that has a great impact on his life. There is really nothing you can do to stop him from taking the vow—he is in love and he is over 18. But what you can do is to open his eyes to the implications of his decision and the things he may not see given his young age.

As discussed before, wisdom is about feeling right from wrong. But for a soon-to-be high school graduate in love, getting married to his sweetheart is all it takes to be happy and therefore seems to be the right thing to do. In this case, use your wisdom and experience to gently guide these young people so they can see the consequence of marrying at such a young age. Apart from financial considerations, they should also consider whether or not they are emotionally ready to be tied down to a family, and most important of all, whether they know each other well enough to be certain that they will be compatible as husband and wife, and as parents to their children. Help your child see what he will miss by giving up a scholarship that will further his education. Help him see himself ten years from graduation, and then let him decide.

If, after having the opportunity to see himself in the crystal ball ten years from now, he still wants to go ahead with the marriage, then he should be taught how to be responsible for the consequences of his own decision, without blaming others or regretting his choice later on. This training for responsible decision-making should start at a very young age. Small children should only be allowed to make small decisions—such as soda or milk; as they grow older it can go up to more serious ones—such as Buddhism or Catholicism.

Western parents usually allow children more freedom to make their own decisions, even though it might not necessarily bring the best results. If children are given the freedom to choose without proper guidance, that very freedom could be hazardous to the child's development. Likewise, Eastern parents who want to be in control of their children for life will also endanger the growth of their children as a person by depriving them of the opportunity to learn how to cultivate wisdom in their decision-making process.

Rewarding Good Behavior

Even when a child is still lying in his crib or sitting in his high chair, parents tend to pay more attention to children who make the wrong decision. Babies lying quietly or toddlers sitting peacefully playing with their toys usually get very little attention, while those crying and throwing a tantrum instantly became the center of attention.

Parents need to pay attention to the good behavior of their children, because if they don't, their children will soon decide to get their attention the wrong way. Making good decisions based on good moral judgment is not easy for young children and they deserve great encouragement. A hug, a kiss, or a smile is all your child wants from you, at least when they are young. This kind of positive response supports them for making the right choices in life. If your child tells you that many of his friends are stealing from the supermarket, do not start to lecture him on how he should stay away from those children, or how bad stealing is. Tell him how happy you are as his parent to know that he is such a wise and sensible child.

Teach your children, starting from when they are quite young, the difference between a wise and an unwise decision. Start by teaching them about consequences or future effects of their actions. That will also train a young child to develop foresight or the ability to look into the future. Children may not have the maturity to see very far, but parents can help to be their binoculars. The young child who steals from his friend's bag should be taught *benevolence* so that he will feel for his friend. He should be taught *wisdom* so that he will think about the consequences of his action. With the right kind of guidance, he would be able to see why it is wrong to steal—he should be able to see his friend looking sad and scared if you explain to your child that the stolen item might mean a lot to him, and himself being interrogated by police or school authorities.

The key is to teach a child from a young age about the criteria for making a good decision. Many adults, who were not given the opportunity to learn how to make decisions, will have a hard time deciding what to do with their lives. And that will be a problem for them when they become parents themselves. This leads us to the next topic about corporal punishment, which is considered right by some parents and wrong by others.

The Damage of Unwise Decisions: Corporal Punishment (Hitting, Slapping, Spanking)

In ancient China, corporal punishment was *the* way to discipline. The cane was highly emphasized and was honored as the "family cane." Children, even adult children, would voluntarily bring the family cane to their father and asked to be punished when they did something that was considered unacceptable. In today's Western world, corporal punishment is viewed as an inappropriate way to discipline and can cause parents to be punished by the law. Children know their rights and many will not put up with any kind of physical punishment.

Many modern parenting authorities blame Confucius for contributing to the authority-oriented social system that justified corporal punishment. As much as I appreciate the wisdom of Confucius, I am afraid that I do not honor his authority-oriented social system and definitely do not validate corporal punishment. Nevertheless, we have to understand that corporal punishment worked for parents in China 5000 years ago, because that was the norm. Children did *not* feel violated by the authority of parents or the caning. Regardless of whether we like the submissive character of these children or not, the lesson we learn here is, corporal punishment is effective *only* if the child concurs with your action. Believe it or not, most Chinese children in ancient times thanked their parents for the punishment, because they genuinely believed that the caning was for their own good.

In today's world, no child will concur with you if you discipline him or her with physical punishment. If children do not genuinely understand and accept your motive, corporal punishment is definitely an act of violence and should never be allowed. It is time instead to again investigate the root and branch. Hitting a child is the branch to two roots: nurture and anger.

The Root Named Nurture

Hitting a child is only one of the many branches serving the root named Nurture. Parents are responsible for nurturing their young children and for protecting them from danger or from being a danger to others. In some situations hitting seems to be the only way to keep your child from getting hurt or from hurting others. However, there are many alternatives that are more effective than hitting a child. Depending on the age of the child, parents can consider the following options, listed in order of child's maturity:

- *Pay Attention to Good Behavior and Ignore Bad Behavior*
  As we discussed in the previous section, if we pay attention
  to a young child playing by himself in his room, he will
  soon know that he will not need to misbehave to get your
  attention.
- *Understand the Real Need Behind a Child's Bad Behavior*
  It may be easier to feed your young child, but letting him
  make a mess while feeding himself is necessary, for he
  needs to learn how to make things work even if it is difficult or more work for you.
- *Teach Your Child to Develop the Right Motive for His or
  Her Actions*
  Fear of punishment, desire for rewards, or determination
  to get attention are immature motives for children, and
  also for adults. Parents should teach children to do what is
  right as opposed to what is wrong. The motivation to do
  what is morally right should be taught to a child from a
  very young age and it will become the root of many of his
  lifelong successes.
- *Communicate With your Child*
  This is actually the only way you can know how to help
  your child to change his bad behavior. You might think
  that your child fights in school because he is a bully but he
  might be doing that just because he is so suppressed by you
  that he wants to cover his fear by attacking others.
- *Set Reasonable Boundaries*
  By setting boundaries, you can teach children the significance of consequences. Children with no boundaries at
  home feel free to do whatever they like at home, in
  school, and in the real world. Children usually have to
  learn the hard way if they are not trained well at home

about how to be responsible for their own actions and accept consequences.

These are just a few of the alternatives to physical punishment. Physical punishment might seem the fastest way to get immediate results when you want to discipline your child. Yet, there is no guarantee that he will learn the lesson, but it is the guaranteed way to break the heart of your child. No matter how you phrase it, you are still violating the dignity of another human being who happens to be weak and helpless because of their age.

Research done by the Family Research Laboratory in the University of New Hampshire (Straus and Paschall) stated that if parents avoid corporal punishment they are more likely to engage in verbal methods of behavior control such as explaining a situation to a child. Increased communication with the child in turn enhances the child's cognitive ability. It also said that the benefits of reduced corporal punishment are likely to include less juvenile delinquency, less adult violence, less masochistic sex, a greater probability of completing higher education, higher income, and lower rates of depression and alcohol abuse (Kaufman, Kanto & Straus 1994; Straus, 1994).

Even if a child who suffered from corporal punishment does not turn out to be violent himself, the suppression by physical force by a parent or parents will often cause the child to overcompensate in their behavior and grow up to be timid, withdrawn, and obedient to all the people around him or her.

The physical and emotional damage caused by physical punishment is obvious. For those parents who do not know the possible effects of physical punishment, it is time to find out before it is too late. For those parents who already know the consequences of physical punishment but do not know how to take other disciplinary measures, it is time to spend more time reading more books on positive discipline. Remember, it is much more strenuous to hit than to read. And for those parents who don't want to do anything about their old habit, please read the following section carefully, because what you need to deal with in your parenting might not be physical punishment . . . it might be child abuse.

The Root Named Anger

We've already discussed how to control our anger with benevolence in chapter 2, but when corporal punishment is one of the branches of this root called anger, parents are actually harming their children because of their own anger. Other branches include verbal abuse that threatens and intimidates the child; neglect that can be as emotionally damaging as other abuses; as well as other tragic acts that we read about in the news.

I always thought that parents spanked, slapped, or hit their child to teach him or her a lesson, but I was wrong. Many years ago when I first started to study parenting, I would share my new knowledge with my friends. I can still remember one ladies luncheon when I was talking about how an angry parent should cool down and take a time-out before they consider any kind of physical punishment. I saw quite a few uneasy looks on the faces of my friends then one of them simply asked, "So what is point of hitting my child if I am not angry anymore?" For a moment, I wanted to slap her so that she could feel *her* humiliation that was caused by *my* anger. But no, just like child abuse, that would bring no positive result. So instead I went through all that I had learned about non-violent discipline, hoping to answer her question in a more civilized way.

If the purpose of slapping, spanking, or hitting your child is simply because you are enraged and you want to hurt your child because he did, or even did not, do something wrong, then your action takes on a whole new significance. It is not an act of punishment; it is an act of violence.

If you are losing control of the situation and suspect you are abusing your child, you should seek professional help before it is too late. It takes great courage to admit your anger, but once you acknowledge the problem and the fear that you feel, you can find help by reaching out to local organizations that help in cases of child abuse, such as Prevent Child Abuse or Parents Anonymous, Inc. Find the courage to admit that you have a problem controlling your anger and seek help from books or support groups. One of the main problems with angry parents is that many find themselves reaching a point where they cannot see anything good in their children or anything bad with hurting them.

Simple Answers to Frequently Asked Questions

WHAT IS WISDOM?

Wisdom, unlike intelligence, is not inborn. Wisdom is what we cultivate inside us, based on knowledge, contemplation, and experience. It enables us to foresee the consequences of our action. To act recklessly is not an act of wisdom.

WHY DO PARENTS NEED WISDOM?

Parents need wisdom because all children are different and parenting is not a one-formula-fits-all process. Success in parenting depends on the result of all of the decisions they make everyday. Wisdom enables them to obtain the best results by making wise decisions in parenting.

WHEN DO WE NEED WISDOM?

We need wisdom whenever we find ourselves at a cross-road and have to discern the right path from the wrong path.

HOW DO WE APPLY WISDOM TO PARENTING?

Here's an example of when we will need to apply discriminating wisdom: You might find yourself in a situation where your six year old is whining and complaining that all his friends have the latest electronic toy and he wants one too. You find it annoying and disturbing. Wisdom teaches us to stop, think, and learn. Learn about the motive of your child and think about how to teach him well. Your child might not really be whining for the toy, he might be whining for attention, power, or just fun. Sometimes children just like to push your buttons so they can see mom and dad jumping up and down. Wisdom will help you show your child that by whining, he will get no attention, no power struggle, and no mom and dad jumping around. You will have to show him that whining will only bring him his parents' disapproval and discipline. Teach him in a calm and firm way how to ask for the things he wants, and help him to learn how to negotiate with good manners. Children are very smart and they will not waste time and energy on behavior that won't bring them results.

Chapter Three

Courage to Make a Difference in Yourself and in the World

COURAGE IS THE FORCE BEHIND ALL THE HARD WORK IN parenting. Just like money and sleep, courage can help to make parenthood a more comfortable experience; yet, too much courage does not necessarily make you a successful parent. You will need to use your courage wisely.

The courage to do the right thing in parenting is important, but what is more important is the courage to strive and persevere when things go wrong. When things aren't perfect, we usually feel battered and tired, it is so much easier to just quit trying and bury our head in the sand. However, just saying "I will persevere" is not enough, because it is so much easier said than done. For critical issues like this, I recommend using our root and branch approach again. If you look at it carefully, the courage to persevere is not the root. Unless we can find out the root or roots that can help to strengthen this branch, it is going to be a very difficult task. In this chapter, we will deal with two roots that will fortify the will power of parents to persevere: *shame and obligation*. Many parenting experts are reluctant to discuss these two words, because they fear that these two words might induce guilt. However, please give yourself a chance to comprehend them and then decide for yourself.

❧ Is Shame Really Necessary? ❧

A man may not be without shame.
When one is ashamed of having been without shame,
he can't be free from feeling shame again.
(Work of Mencius, bk vii, pt. 1, ch. vii)

We are sorry each time we regret doing something wrong by choice or by accident, but we only feel shameful when we consider our choice to be morally wrong. In other words, a person with no moral values at all will never feel shame. But it takes more than just having a sense of moral values to do the right thing. A person with a good sense of ethics can still deny the feeling of shame because he or she decides to.

For example, people know it is morally wrong to cheat on their spouses but some do it anyway because they claim that their spouse is the one at fault. It is also the same with parents who abuse or neglect their children and then claim that their children are the ones to blame. Not only is hurting a helpless child unwise, but it is shamefully wrong—no matter how an individual might try to make it look and sound better. Common rationalizations for this immoral behavior include: "That is the only way to make him learn." "It is our culture to spank naughty children." "My parents hit me all the time." "He asked for it." These are all fabricated reasons parents give themselves to avoid the feeling of shame. However, denying the sense of shame inside will only allow these individuals to turn their heads away from the truth, and in doing that, they give up the strength and power that shame can generate which can help them find a better way to respond. We need only be sorry if we unintentionally hurt our children with our mistakes—yes, parents *do* make mistakes. But we should feel shame if we already know about the mistake and keep doing it. In short, shame is involved when we *choose* to hurt others, or ourselves, physically or mentally, and that is something children should also be taught from a young age.

Teaching Shame to Your Children

Lead the people with political maneuvers and keep them orderly with punishment, and they will avoid punishments but will be without a sense of shame. Lead them with virtue and keep them orderly through observing ritual, and they will develop a sense of shame, and moreover, will order themselves. (Analects 2.3)

Confucius considered shame to be more effective than punishment. Shame is something that needs to be taught and cultivated like other virtues. The *Merriam-Webster Dictionary* defines *shame* as "a painful sense of having done something wrong." Believe it or not, all children do have this "painful sense" from a very young age, but if it is not cultivated, it will fade away. Young children are instinctively sensitive of the pain of other people; even a toddler knows something is wrong when he sees tears in your eyes. The earlier a parent can help a child feel other people's pain, the earlier a child will feel shame inside themselves when they cause the pain in other people. This could actually be the best counterforce for the violence that surrounds us nowadays.

In order to teach shame to our children we must honestly and openly discuss our feelings. Here's an example.

Betty was staying in the car when her fifteen-year-old daughter Kelly went inside a coffee shop to buy coffee and a bagel. She usually did not like the coffee from this particular shop, but since she was feeling a little hungry that day she decided to go in and get a muffin.

As Betty was checking out the pastries inside the glass case, she saw Kelly in the far corner of the coffee shop with a woman in her twenties. Betty was about to go over to say hello when she saw Kelly give something to this woman, who in return gave some money to Kelly. Betty became anxious and very curious of what was going on. She took a deep breath and walked over.

Kelly looked shocked and frightened to see her mother but had no choice but let her mother check out the paper bag. Inside was a pair of earrings. Betty was very relieved it was not drugs, but when she looked again, she knew it was not too far from what she feared.

It was a pair of gold earrings that looked exactly like the pair she had lost last week. Her daughter had stolen her earrings and was trading it for money from this woman. Betty did not say anything and just walked back out to her car.

She was heartbroken. Her daughter had stolen from her and had shattered her dream that her daughter was honest and trustworthy. Shouting and yelling and punishing Kelly would only make her defensive. Kelly must know that it was wrong to steal and yet she had chosen to do so. Betty would have to start with investigating the knowledge; she would have to listen very carefully to Kelly's explanation.

It turned out that Kelly knew this woman through another friend who was making good money by selling her mom's jewelry. Kelly said she never did that before and that she was doing it now because she really liked a designer handbag that was popular among her friends. Betty was angry when she heard Kelly's confession, but she knew that she had to take courage and stop herself from yelling and shouting at her daughter. Kelly, in fact, did know that it was wrong to steal, but she had chosen to do the wrong thing because she thought she could get away with it.

What would courage look like in this situation? Betty would have to have courage to stop and consider the whole situation before she responds. She would have to understand that Kelly really could have gotten away with it if she had not be hungry and went inside this coffee shop. She would also have to understand that if Kelly wants to steal behind her back, there is really nothing she, or even the law, could do to stop her from trying to steal. The only thing that will safeguard Kelly from stealing again will be by cultivating her own sense of shame, and making her feel the shame inside herself. Some might say that shame is bad for the self-esteem of a child, but shame helps cultivate an innate positive moral standard. What is more important in a child, indiscriminate good self-esteem or a strong moral standard? The decision is yours.

Another thing that is important in a situation like this is to let the child knows about the pain that she is causing you. No one likes to be hurt, especially by someone you love. If your child loves you, and only if she loves you, feeling your pain can be the best punishment for her. It is important for you to share with your children, even very young ones, the "painful sense of doing something wrong." If you yell at them just because you had a bad day, tell them that you did not mean to hurt them and that you are sorry. And every time they hurt you, express to them that it is painful to be hurt by them. Sometimes just a sad look will make a young child understand your pain. If you do not train your child from a young age, you really cannot blame him for rebelling and causing you pain without feeling shame and remorse when they are old enough to be responsible for themselves.

But be careful: If shame is over-used or used improperly, it will be very damaging to a child's self-esteem, self-confidence, and self-image. *You will need to use shame carefully as a tool to teach, and not as a way to hurt.* Many Chinese parents like to use shame to insult a child so that he won't dare to make the same mistake again. Little do they know that if they do not show respect to the child when they deliver the message, they will only humiliate him and force him to believe that he is worthless and that he can't do anything right. Eventually his negative thoughts will drive him to becoming what he believes in.

The key here again is in the balance between too much shame and no shame at all. Eastern parents will need to understand the damaging effects of inducing, in a harsh way, too much shame in a child, while Western parents will need to educate children about this self-regulatory force. You must teach a child to be his own judge. The same goes for parents: Parents must become better judges of what they do to their children.

Nobody likes to feel shameful; it is a very uncomfortable, if not painful, feeling. It actually takes more courage for parents to allow themselves to feel shame for what they have done to their children than for them to lie to themselves about their innocence. Can we honestly say that our children's problems have nothing to do with us or that we can't do anything else to help them? Though it is hard for parents to acknowledge the feeling of shame inside themselves, it is worth every bit of effort because this feeling is the root that will allow our courage to persevere. What can give you more power to change than the will to get rid of a "painful sense?"

❧ OBLIGATION MEANS LESS PERSONAL FREEDOM ❦

To persevere is courageous in a parent. In order to cultivate the courage to persevere so as to reach your goals in parenting, it is important to study and understand the second root of courage: The recognition of obligation.

Confucius said that the parent/child relationship is one of the most important among the five human relationships—the relationships between king and minister, parent and child, sibling and sibling, husband and wife, and friend and friend. How each person plays his or her role in these five relationships is important to the well-being of society, which will affect the peace and prosperity of the country.

The virtue to enforce obligation in human relationships is *chung*, which means "dutiful" in English. This virtue teaches a person about his or her obligation to do his or her best in each of the five human relationships. Parents who pursue only personal freedom and individual choices might not like the term "obligation." However, ignoring one's obligation as a parent is giving in to selfishness and to personal gains at the expense of those who are helpless and at our mercy.

Confucius wrote pages and pages about how a child should be obligated to serve his parents—a virtue called filial piety—but much less about the obligation of a parent. I believe this is because the obligation of a parent to raise child well has always been viewed as a natural duty in China. Confucius made the natural love and obligation between members of the family the basis of a general morality and the first and most important relationship within the family is the relationship between a parent and a child.

The Obligation to Do Our Best

The reason why obligation is so important in parenting is because it will determine whether or not you are willing to take courage and deal with the many problems you will encounter throughout your parenthood. Consider these examples that show what it means to respond to an obligation that is greater than one's own desires.

> *Tom is a US Army Reservist who owns a small grocery store in a suburban town in Indiana. He was really excited when he heard the news that his wife was pregnant with their first child. Then he received notification that he would need to leave for Iraq in two month's time. He worried that his pregnant wife would not be able to handle the work in the store all by herself while he was not around. He worried that he would not be around to see and help with the birth of his first child. He also feared that he might not ever be able to see his child. So many worries and fears, and yet he knew he had no choice. He decided it was his obligation to serve his country even though he was reluctant to leave his family behind.*

> *Martha had worked a long night. She was finally fast asleep at 1 A.M. when the phone rang. It was her best friend Judy and she was sounding even more lifeless*

than the half-asleep Martha. Judy's husband had just left her for another woman and Judy said she felt like killing herself. Martha was very tired, but Judy's sob instantly woke her up. She knew Judy should not be by herself at a moment like this. She got dressed quickly and drove to the other side of town to her friend's house. Even though it was a cold and snowy night and Martha would have loved to sleep in her warm and comfortable bed, she did not hesitate for a moment because she felt that it was her obligation to be there for her good friend.

The sense of obligation to something greater than ourselves gives us courage to do what we don't want to do. It is what makes Tom leave his family and go to war, and what makes Martha jump out of her comfortable bed to help her friend. This is the same courage that parents need to persevere when things get out of hand with their children. If parents do not feel that they are obligated to care and protect their own children, it will be easy for them to turn their heads and look away from problems as they arise and even give up when their children get into trouble. It is only when parents feel their obligation toward their children that they will take courage and keep trying to help.

The virtue of courage must work hand in hand with the virtue of chung throughout the journey of parenting. Having courage with no sense of obligation when things get difficult will be like fighting a battle without spirit and conviction in the cause. Without the spirit to fight—and trust me, it sometimes really feels like a war—it is so easy to just give up and throw away all the helpful parenting books. In today's world, the spirit to fight lies in the preservation of chung, which helps us hold on to our obligation to our children through thick and thin.

I have changed a lot since I started to incorporate these virtues into my parenting experience. However, there are still times when my short-fused character turns me back into the unwise parent I used to be. Those are the times that I need the courage to feel the shame. It is a painful feeling, but it is strong enough to make me work hard to avoid making the same mistake again. As for obligation, for a temperamental and impatient person like me, if I did not have the courage to hold on to the obligation to be the best mother I know how, my engine would have stopped long time ago.

Simple Answers to Frequently Asked Questions

WHAT IS COURAGE?

Courage is the inner strength to do what is right, despite hardship and difficulties.

WHY DO PARENTS NEED COURAGE IN PARENTING?

Parents need courage to give them the strength to conquer the fear inside them. Common fears include fear of change, fear of losing control, and fear of letting go.

WHEN DO WE NEED COURAGE?

We need courage when we need more inner strength to choose the right way and not the easy way. We also need courage to strive and persevere even when things are more difficult than expected.

HOW DO WE APPLY COURAGE TO PARENTING?

Here's an example of how to apply courage to parenting. Your fifteen-year-old daughter is interested in attending a language program in France for the summer. You are worried about her going because she has never traveled on her own. Be very careful and check the credibility and competency of the institution that will sponsor her, but take courage to allow your child to broaden her horizon. This experience will help her gain confidence and independence. Give credit to your child for her courage, for wanting to explore a world outside of her comfort zone. You might end up with a few sleepless nights when your daughter is away, but knowing that you have provided her with such a good learning opportunity should make you feel proud of your own courage.

PART TWO

The Three Roles of a Virtuous Parent

Now that we've discussed the three universal virtues and the attributes and actions of those virtues, let's look more deeply at what we can do with them. How do they really fit in with our roles as a parent? Just like our role as a citizen of the world, the role of a parent is one that we have no choice but to play well. You can quit school, quit work, quit your marriage, but you cannot, or should not, quit the role of a parent.

What is exactly the role of a parent? Before we assume we know what that role is, let us stop and consider it. This will help us cultivate the virtues we need to respond to all our parenting obligations. The simplest definition of the role of the parent is "to raise a child." But the role of parenting has evolved over time from raising a child inside a simple village to raising a child in today's complex world. With the development of telecommunications and the fall of the autocratic parenting system, parenting is more complicated than ever. Parents now need different skills to allow our children the freedom that our cultural climate requires, while, at the same time, staying in control for our children's safety and well-being.

The three roles for a parent as described in this section—the Ruler, the Teacher, and the Friend—reflect the active roles that each of the three virtues embody. These roles are like the three hats that a parent needs to put on, one at a time, in every day parenting. Each role needs to be interchanged from time to time to accommodate any different situations. But remember, though our role may change from time to time, our love and our virtues should be constant and are necessary when we wear any one of these hats.

❦ THE ROLE OF A RULER ❦

I use the term ruler instead of leader or governor because a ruler represents absolute authority. Throughout parenthood, there are many occasions when we need to have absolute say over our children's behavior. For example, when your toddler wants to play with fire or when your teenagers drink and drive, you need to be absolutely firm with your rules.

Nevertheless, it does not mean that a ruler can use absolute authority whenever they feel like it. In *Da Xue* or *The Great Learning* Confucius set forth the principles of moral science, which are to be applied in the conduct of the government. He stressed that "a ruler who takes charge of a nation cannot afford to be careless, for if he is not cautious and deviates from the true path and becomes mean and self-centered, he will be overthrown and will lose his empire." The true path in here starts with the cultivation of benevolence. Benevolent parent-rulers will gain the trust of their children.

❦ THE ROLE OF A TEACHER ❦

No parent can deny their role as a teacher in the lives of their children. Confucius had been honored as the "Foremost Teacher" and "The Teacher of all Seasons" in China and in many corners of the world for over two thousand years. For Confucius, teachers should be inspiring and respectful. It is more important to teach a student to think than to teach them what to do. To be a wise teacher yourself is as important as teaching your student to be a wise student. Wise parent-teachers will gain the respect of their children.

❦ THE ROLE OF A FRIEND ❦

Many people think that to be your child's friend is the easiest way to parent. Unfortunately, they are wrong. A child that grows up with no guidance from his parent-ruler or parent-teacher but only with friendliness from his "friendly" parent will become an adult who knows nothing about how to nurture a good relationship with *anyone*, including his parents. It might give us superficial pleasure to act like a friend to our children, but it will not serve our children or ourselves well. However, when the moment is right, be ready to play the role of friend, even though it will take great courage to let go and see your child learn on his own. Courageous parent-friends will gain the heart of their children.

❦ WHEN TO PLAY EACH ROLE ❦

Playing the wrong role at the wrong time can be dangerous. Though we should always keep the three universal virtues close to our hearts, the role of ruler, teacher, and friend are the three roles that can help us parent effectively in everyday situations. The simplest way to answer the question "How do I know when to wear which hat?" is to ask yourself "What do I want to achieve with my action?" *If the answer is to discipline or safeguard your child, you need your ruler hat. If the answer is to teach and inspire your child, you need your teacher hat. If the answer is to be there for your child and provide him with your support and companionship, you need your friend hat.* As a rule of thumb, the younger the child, the more you should wear the ruler and teacher hats; as the child grows older, you should be wearing your friend hat most of the time.

Chapter Four

The Benevolent Ruler: To Rule and to Love

WHEN IT COMES TO PROVIDING FOR AND SAFEGUARDING OUR children, being a parent means more than being a leader or a guardian. We play the ruler when we need to protect and discipline our children. Our role here is to use whatever reasonable way we can to tell our children the rules of life. Being the ruler does not mean that we have to be autocratic and mean; we need to be benevolent rulers to our children—rulers who rule with their hearts.

❀ DEMOCRACY AND BENEVOLENT AUTHORITY ❀

When a citizen can handle freedom and responsibility, let him have freedom; When a citizen is not ready to handle freedom and responsibility, teach him first. (Analects 8.9)

Rulers should always be in control but not necessarily controlling. Democracy calls for equality and rule by the people. Confucius believed that only those who are capable of handling the freedom to choose should be allowed to choose for themselves. In other words, those not capable should follow the rule until they are capable to do so. A good ruler is responsible to lead and act in such a way that the people will be nourished, protected, and educated. This quote can also be translated to *"Citizens can be made to follow direction, but not to understand it."* Until today, there is still argument as to which definition is the true meaning of the text. Nevertheless, I think both definitions can be applied to today's parenting with the latter more applicable to younger children.

As parents we have to choose the right method between begging and commanding to get our children to comply with our rules. One thing that is constant, however, is that no matter what method we use, we want to change our child's mind when he makes, or is about to make, a mistake. We want him to behave in ways acceptable to our standards now and in the future. In other words, we want our children to follow our guidance. This requires the obedience of the child. Therefore, the root of the authority issue is actually obedience, more than it is power or control, even though it might not seem so on the surface.

Obedience is Not a Bad Thing

We need the status of an authority to get the obedience of a child. Many western parenting experts do not like the use of words like "authority" and "obedience," but the bottom line is if you want to guide your child well, you will need him to obey your authority. To do this effectively, you will have to balance your authority with benevolence. Confucius stressed the *middle way* or the balance of extremes. If you are a benevolent authority figure who gains the trust and respect of your child, obedience will naturally follow. If you are an authority figure and show no benevolence, your children will despise your authority and will rebel. Today, when citizens are allowed to challenge even the authority of the President, obedience to authority should never be taken in an extreme way at home, and parents should not raise a child who knows only obedience and never dares to appropriately challenge or question authority.

If you cannot decide whether or not you should be considered the authority in the house, you'd better do some serious thinking fast. For if you want to be considered an equal with your children, it won't be long before you will find out that you and your children can never be equals. Before you know it, they will be the authority in the family and looking for *your* obedience. Look around modern American families and you will see what I mean and the negative consequences of this inappropriate relationship.

❧ THE ACTIONS OF A BENEVOLENT RULER ❧

How can a ruler be in control and not controlling? The key is in how people *feel* when they submit to the ruling. Do they feel benevolence or do they feel might? Rule by benevolence uses love and humanity while rule by might uses force and violence, which sometimes is presented to people as superficial benevolence. Thousands of children are abused everyday in the name of love because it is not easy for parents to admit that they hurt their children just because they had a bad day or that they had no other way to discipline them. When a ruler pretends that he is using benevolence while actually using force to subdue his subjects, the people do not genuinely submit to him in their hearts; rather, they submit in a superficial way just because they do not have enough strength to resist. On the other hand, if a virtuous ruler practices benevolence, his subjects will submit to his rule with their hearts. When we play the role of a ruler with our children, it is very important for us to be able to win their hearts, because if we lose their hearts, our children will become resentful even to the point of open rebellion.

Understanding
To be a ruler is difficult, but to be a subject is not easy either.
(Analects 13.15)

Confucius believed that it is important to understand the problems your subjects are facing before you can have success with your rule. It is always easy to be the judge when you only have to listen to the story of the defendant or accuser. But it will never be a fair trial. The same goes for your rule at home. When a child presents a case to you and you have to be the one to make the decision, you will need to suspend your ruling until you have investigated the whole truth from all angles. Here's an example.

> *Robyn hates middle school because all the girls are so judgmental of each other and they love to gang up on her. They tease Robyn about her weight and call her names and tell her that fat people are losers.*
>
> *Robyn has tried to talk to her mother, Tammy, about the problem, but Tammy is also overweight, and Robin's immature way of explaining the situation often makes her mother become defensive of her own obesity. Tammy often ends up accusing her daughter of being too sensitive and overly concerned with what other people say about her. When Robyn starts to dramatically cut down her food intake, Tammy realizes that it is time to put on her ruler hat and stop what looks like the onset of an eating disorder.*

First of all, a mother-ruler will need to understand that she needs to be a cushion and not a brick wall to a daughter in this kind of situation. As we can see, Robyn has had enough brick walls in school that are crushing her already. Second, Tammy must understand the pain Robyn is going through and that she really does not mean to offend her mom. Third, Tammy must understand that Robyn is too young to know the difference between the accusation and the truth. Robyn must understand that what her friends said about fat people is not true. As a mother, Tammy must straighten out the teasing by telling Robyn about all the people who are overweight and yet successful and popular in life. Last but not least, a mother-ruler must acknowledge Robyn's concerns and seek professional help so she can lose weight in a healthy and sensible way. It might even be a good opportunity for them to go on a weight loss program together.

Teasing is a big problem in middle or even junior high schools, especially amongst girls who can be very mean to one another. If parents and school authorities are only concerned about the academic problems a child faces in school, a child of a young age can often feel lost and helpless when the problem involves human relationships in school.

Children are young. Their sense of time is different and, generally, they just want to get results fast. They haven't developed the maturity to think of the consequences of some of their actions. As a ruler, you need to be there to stop them from making silly mistakes. Eating disorders, lying about their family background, fighting back physically, or even exacting revenge with violence are all "methods" that children think will help them stop mean ridicule from children who have never been taught about benevolence at home or in school. As a good parent-ruler, you should be on guard and rule with benevolence so that you will be able to participate in their strategy planning as they confront such difficult situations in life.

Be a Good Role Model

If rulers are proper in their own conduct, subjects will follow suit without need of command. But if they are not proper, even when they command, others will not obey.
(Analects 13.6)

Confucius made a point when he said that a ruler's own behavior was more influential than the rules they made. Even though most children do not consider their parents to be their role models, a parent's influence on a child is phenomenal. Consider this example.

> *Paul had great trouble getting Katrina, his twelve-year-old daughter, to be kind to her five-year-old brother. Katrina was a nice girl. Usually she was kind and gentle but, for some reason, she never was kind or gentle to her younger brother. She was mean to him, and sometimes even hit him. Paul always thought that elder sisters should love and take good care of their younger siblings. He had tried to use punishment to stop Katrina's behavior, but it did not seem to work*
>
> *Paul finally decided to talk to Katrina. He hoped he might learn something about the root of her hostility with her brother. Katrina admitted that she also felt kind of bad for being a mean sister but she didn't think that jealousy or sibling rivalry was the reason. She also didn't think that she disliked her brother, but she just felt that it was okay to be authoritative with him. Then she expressed that she did not understand what was*

wrong with her behavior since her father was always rude and blunt to his younger brother who just lived a few blocks away from them. Katrina just thought that maybe that's the way siblings should behave toward each other. As for the hitting, that was what her parents did to her when they tried to discipline her.

Paul had overlooked the fact that no matter how he had tried to teach Katrina to be a good sister to her brother, what she observed in his behavior, both with his own brother and in the way he treated her, spoke louder than any thing he said.

Children learn from examples. If you want them to be well-mannered, hardworking, honest, responsible, and compassionate, you'll need to be well-mannered, hardworking, honest, responsible, and compassionate yourself. You will have to walk your talk, if not, you will have to think of a very good answer when your child asks you "Why can you do it and I can't?" If Paul wants Katrina to treat her brother kindly, it is time for him to put on the ruler hat and demonstrate benevolence by practicing it in his own life.

❧ GAIN TRUST, NOT FEAR ❧

A benevolent person will only ask his subject to work hard after gaining their trust. Without trust, the people will think that they are being ill treated.
(Analects 19.10)

When wearing the ruler hat, it is very easy to make your children feel like you are dominating, controlling, and unreasonable. The reason is because it is your job to set rules that can help them lead a healthy, safe, and moral life. Unfortunately, these are usually things that do not appeal to children. You'll have to understand that you are actually making them do things that they do not like to do. As a parent-ruler, you will want to gain the trust and allegiance of your child by proving to him that you love him and that you are doing the right thing for his sake. Not because you are bossy and not because you are angry, but because you know what is best for your child.

Your two-year-old son will definitely prefer candy to healthy food; your fourteen-year-old daughter will rather watch TV than study chemistry; your eleven-year-old son will take out the garbage or do other chores only when he feels like helping out in the house not necessarily when you tell him to; and your three-year-old daughter will like to kick whoever tries to play with her favorite toy. It's important to teach your kids that these things are not acceptable—for a reason.

> Raise up the true and place them over the crooked,
> and theallegiance of the people will be yours.
> (Analects 2.19)

This seed of trust and allegiance will need to be planted in your child's heart at the early stage of parenthood. The earlier you plant the seed, the easier it will grow. Trust cannot be taught to a child, it will have to be gained. In order to gain trust, it's important that we are upright, fair, and just when telling our children what is right and what is wrong, even when they are very young. But just as trust can be gained, it can also be lost so it is important for you to avoid behaviors that will make your child lose her trust in you.

✦ THE FIVE WONDERS OF A BENEVOLENT RULER ✦

The five wonders in governing are:
  1. *Be generous in benefiting your subject but do not be extravagant.*
  2. *Make your subject work hard but do not incur ill will.*
  3. *Desire for benevolence not power.*
  4. *Be poised but not arrogant.*
  5. *Be dignified but not fierce.* (Analects 20.2)

The role of the ruler is probably the hardest role to play in parenthood. To be a benevolent ruler you must be able to stop your child from hurting himself with things he likes to do, and make him do things that are good for him but not necessarily liked by him. This means that the rules of a parent-ruler will have to be carefully selected, and you will have to stand by your rules even if they cause you embarrassment in public or resentment at home. *A benevolent ruler will need the virtue of benevolence to set the rules; the virtue of wisdom to know if there is anything wrong with the rules; and the virtue of courage to carry out the rules even when they are difficult to enforce.*

Confucius laid out five "wonders" for ruling with benevolence. Try to follow these guidelines when playing the role of a benevolent ruler.

1. Be Generous

Be generous with your time and attention and find out what will benefit your children in terms of their physical, emotional, and intellectual growth. Leading them the right direction will be the best gift you can give. Being extravagant with material gifts will only buy their superficial compliance and will prove harmful to your child's well-being.

We often hear people complained that they do not have enough time for their children. They give reasons such as: they need to spend time with office work, housework, social activities, or any other activities that they think needs their attention more than their children do. To children, especially young children, there is really no better gift parents can give than their time and attention. Many parents work hard so that the family will live better, but what does a big beautiful house give to a child when they always feel lonely inside? In fact, what does a big beautiful house give to us when we hardly know the children who live in the house with us? Big houses or fancy cars can all come and go. A child's desire to be loved by you will never return once they have given it up. Think for a moment: What is taking you away from your children? Are these other demands really more important to you than the love of your child? Be generous with your time and love, and your children will be generous in return.

2. Make Children Work Hard

It is important to make children work hard for the things they want to achieve. Some parents are afraid to make their children work hard because they're afraid that their children might dislike them for it. Find out the interests of your children and allow them to work hard according to their interest. In this way, even if they find it hard work, they will not have ill will.

By working hard, children will learn to treasure what they have worked hard for. As a parent-ruler, we should encourage children to reach for the stars. Give them a chance to develop new interests in sports, music, art, or any other activities. Children seldom know where their interests and talents are when they are young, and are usually reluctant to try new things. Parent-ruler should give them a push, but never demand result by might.

3. Benevolence vs. Might

Parent-rulers who are able to instill benevolence will feel contented and abundant. Parents who desire power will become controlling parents who always feel discontented.

A parent-ruler who desires power will always end up in a power struggle with their children. As the children grow older, they will find out that their might is losing its power. Many will try to maintain in control by escalating the force they apply. The result can be disturbing. Benevolence, on the other hand, helps a parent to stay away from power struggles. When there is a conflict, a benevolent ruler will be able to see the whole picture from all angles. The desire will be to love the child and make his life better for him instead of making oneself more powerful.

4. Be Poised but Not Arrogant

You need to show your child that you are confident and poised. You also need to let your children know that even though you are the authority, you are not arrogant and will not belittle them. Being arrogant will only drive your child away from you.

Being a poised and self-assured parent-ruler is good, for then we will gain the respect of our children. However, there is a fine line between looking poised and appearing arrogant. If we look as if we always "know it all" and that our children know nothing, our children will feel intimidated and will not even approach us for guidance.

Sometimes we forget how "big" we appear to young children—they actually have to look up to see our faces. And even when they are as tall, or even taller, than us they still see us as someone higher on the hierarchy ladder. In other words, children do feel inferior to us even though they may not look that way. A parent-ruler should never forget to see how she looks in the eyes of her child.

5. Be Dignified but Not Fierce

The parent-ruler should not scare children like Snow White's stepmother or Count Dracula. Parents need to gain the respect of their children by being dignified and respectful. That is the only way your children will look up to you and respect your authority.

No matter how friendly we are with our children, we should always be someone they look up to. The image of parent-ruler in the mind of our children should be someone who is dignified and respectful, but at the same time, someone who is nice to be with.

If children feel that you are fierce and temperamental, they will never know when it is safe to approach you. The fear factor will stop them from coming close to you, physically and mentally, and they will be reluctant to communicate and seek help from you. As a person, you will be viewed as a bully, and as a parent, you will be seen as a tyrant.

❧ RULING LIKE THE WIND AND GRASS ❧

When Ji Kang Zi was consulting Confucius about governing, he asked, "To execute the trouble makers so that it would be orderly, how does that sound?"

*Confucius said, "When governing, why seek to kill? If
you aim for goodness, the masses will be good. Virtue of
the noble leader is like the wind, and that of the subjects is like the grass. Grass will bend when the wind
sweeps over them.* (Analects 12.19)

"Wind" here means a trend or movement that can influence
the behavior of the followers. Confucius is telling us that the
virtue of a ruler can be as powerful as the wind; when the wind
blows, the subjects will "bend" and follow in the same direction. Virtue will then become the popular culture that will
change the way your subject thinks and behaves. Punishment
will then be unnecessary because people will behave properly
not because of the fear of punishment, but because they have
learned about right and wrong. When you rule with virtue,
your subjects will understand virtue. Consider this example.

*Anthony was shocked when the principal from her
daughter's school called and told him that Maggie, his
twelve-year-old, was found cheating on her biology
exam. Anthony knew that Maggie wanted to do well in
school, but what made her so desperate to achieve even
at the expense of a disciplinary suspension?*

*Maggie looked nervous and scared when her par-
ents asked her about the cheating incident. She said she
was not the only one who cheated, and that it was just
bad luck that she got caught. Maggie said that she and
her group of friends actually planned how to cheat weeks
before the exam. Many of them spent more time planning
their cheating tactics than they did actually studying.*

*Anthony and his wife had learned about active lis-
tening, and so they were able to do a good job getting*

as much information from Maggie as possible. When asked the big question, "Why cheat?" Maggie looked at her parents and slowly said, "Why not? Parents all cheat one way or another."

Then she started to tell her parents what her friends' parents did: They cheated on each other, cheated at work, cheated on their taxes, told lies to get what they wanted. She gave many other examples of the way adults cheat. When asked if she ever found her parents cheating, Maggie said, "Didn't you cheat at the restaurant the other day when they gave you the wrong bill and you paid it anyway? Weren't you happy that you had saved over $30?"

Moral values cannot be taught by words only. Parents will have to demonstrate good values like the wind so that their children will bend naturally with no resistance.

In Chinese writing, "trend" consists of two words, "wind" and "air." Both words stand for something that is not visible and yet that is most powerful in our daily life. Parents are like the trendsetters in a family and it will take many trendsetters to make virtuous living a popular trend that will impact the world like the wind impacts the grass.

All through this chapter, we have stressed the importance of being a benevolent ruler in the lives of our children. Even though benevolence is also important in the other two roles, which we will discuss in the following two chapters, it is essential for the parent-ruler to understand the hidden power of benevolence in a world where power is always identified with force and might. Unfortunately, force and might will often bring about resistance and revenge within the heart of any human being.

Simple Answers to Frequently Asked Questions

WHAT IS A PARENT-RULER?

A parent-ruler is one whose role is to rule the child so that she will be free from harm. This role calls for absolute obedience from the child who is not yet capable of making the right decision on her own because of her immaturity.

WHY DO PARENT-RULERS NEED TO BE BENEVOLENT?

A ruler is a person of authority. If a ruler is not benevolent, children will not feel the love behind the rule, but instead, will feel the suppression that they hate. A benevolent ruler rules by trust and allegiance and not by might.

WHEN DO WE NEED TO PLAY THE ROLE OF A RULER IN OUR PARENTING?

We should put on our ruler hat when we need to be in control and protect our children from harm. We should play the ruler role with discretion, for it is not wise to overuse the authority of a parent-ruler. Parents who associate themselves as a fulltime ruler will raise either submissive or rebellious children.

HOW SHOULD A BENEVOLENT PARENT-RULER RULE?

Consider this example: When the doctor tells you that furry animals and stuffed toys are hazardous to your child's health because she is asthmatic, you know that your child will still fight to keep her stuffed animal collection in her room. Consider yourself lucky if she does not have a real furry animal!

A benevolent parent-ruler will have to be firm and rule against a child's will when the child is too young to see the significance of the health hazard involved. It is distressing to see the tears of a sad child when we need to take away her favorite toys, but be kind and gentle and explain to her that it breaks your heart to see her suffer from asthma, and that you have to do anything possible to protect her from harm. Put all her stuffed toys in a nice container, do not throw them away, and let her know that she can visit them any time and that she can have them back in the future. A benevolent ruler should always rule in a kind but firm way.

Chapter Five

The Wise Teacher:
To Teach and to Inspire

WHILE THE RULER ROLE HAS YOU WORK TOWARD GAINING THE *trust* of your children, the Teacher role has you work toward gaining *respect* from them. It is the most used role in parenting, and one that we start playing almost immediately after we become a parent. First we teach our newborn child how to love by holding him in our arms and making him feel cherished and secure. We then teach him how to walk, talk, and behave. All of these lessons are so important in the development of a child, but we soon learn that what we teach our children only takes hold if we know how to send the message so that it is received on the other end. For over five thousand years, Confucius has been greatly respected as the "Teacher of Teachers." We can learn a lot about teaching by studying how Confucius taught his students and what he said about being a good teacher.

❧ WORDS OR NO WORDS ❧

In expressing oneself, it is simply a matter
of getting the point across. (Analects 15.41)

This is such an important point to remember when we put on our teacher hat. Children seem to have radar that can detect the coming of a long lecture. They have no choice but listen if they are in a classroom, even though they still have the liberty to daydream or even fall asleep. But once outside the classroom, we may have to work very hard to get their attention.

Whenever you put on your teacher hat, think of yourself as the producer of a TV commercial. You have one minute to do your talk and you have to get to the point fast. Think of your child as holding a remote control with his finger right on the control buttons. Don't forget that you do have your right to teach them, but they also have the ability to block off your messages. *A teacher's words will need to be simple, clear, and direct, so that the message is effectively and clearly conveyed.* A lot of children will give their parents an indication when their message is too long or too repetitive. Cues like "Okay, okay" or "You've said that already" usually means it's time to switch the channel. Once you hear the cues that your child has understood what you are trying to say, stop. If she agrees with you, hearing it one time is enough, and if she does not agree, repeating your message many more times really does not help. Give her a chance to tell you what she has to say . . . and listen carefully. A good teacher does not only teach. A good teacher also listens and considers a student's viewpoint.

The timing for talking to your child is also very important. Do not talk to them while they are watching TV, using the computer, or listening to music. Talking with your child requires concentration on both sides because, hopefully, it is a time when both of you will be listening carefully and thinking about what is being said.

❧ TEACH THROUGH YOUR ACTIONS ❧

Confucius said, "I think I have said enough."
Zi Gong asked, "If teacher does not speak, what will
we students learn and discuss?"
Confucius said, "What has heaven said? The seasons
come and go, and everything grows and fades, but
what has heaven said?" (Analects 17.19)

Many of us are not aware of the fact that the art of teaching is not only based on the words we say, but on our behavior and morality. Our children will learn a lot from us just by being with us. Even before your baby understands a word you say, your touches, your smiles, and your frowns all speak to him. When he grows older, he will start to imitate you without instruction. You can learn a lot about your own facial expressions and body gestures by looking at a young child. Children usually don't like to do what you tell them to, such as "close your mouth when you chew" or "cover your nose when you sneeze." But they will be the first ones to imitate things that you may not even realize you are doing, such as frowning, biting your fingernails, shrugging your shoulders, or shaking your leg.

How you speak and treat others will also teach your child every day. If you think of it this way, parents are actually wearing their teacher hat *all the time.* It might be a scary thought for many, but what you dislike in your child might actually be there because he has been a good student of yours. Students learn from their schoolteacher during class time, but they learn from their parent-teacher twenty-four hours a day. So if there is something in you that you do not like to see in your child, the only way is for you to change it in yourself first. A parent who is always late cannot expect her child to be punctual and time conscious. A father who beats up his wife and children cannot expect his children to be kind and caring to the people around them.

❧ DON'T DISCRIMINATE ❧

I teach everyone without discrimination.
(Analects 15.39)

Confucius was the first teacher in China who promoted education with "no discrimination"—he believed that education should be for everyone, not just for the rich and privileged. He said that for him it was education that classified people, not money or hereditary aristocracy. With this emphasis on education, the quality of the teacher becomes much more important.

In order to be a good teacher, you must understand the differences between your students and accept those differences even if they are not what you desire. As a parent-teacher you may find things in your child that do not meet your expectations. This gets even more complicated if you have more than one child, because consciously or unconsciously you will start to compare them, just as you would students in a class. One of your children might be academically talented and waltz his way into big name schools with no problem, while your other child might be artistically talented but struggling with his academic classes. A good parent-teacher will see that a child's talent has nothing to do with being a good child; they will just have to be taught in different ways. If taught properly, they will both turn out to be good sons or daughters, who will achieve in their own special way.

You may find that your children have totally different temperaments. One child could be gentle and easy going while the other child could be temperamental and aggressive. It does not mean that one is better than the other. As a wise teacher, you will have to help each one of them to develop their strength and improve on their weakness. Motivate the gentle and easy-going child to be more aggressive and competitive, and calm the aggressive child so that she will find tranquility and peace in life.

❧ HAVE THE RIGHT APPROACH ❦

As described by one of Confucius' students,
"The master was always gentle yet firm, commanding
but not harsh, dignified and calm." (Analects 7.38)

As described earlier, *how* you teach is as important, if not more important, than *what* you teach. For many parents, being gentle and calm comes naturally. For the rest of us, it can be as hard as making ourselves walk on our heels. The key to success is knowing the urgency and importance of the situation, in this case, the importance of parenting with the right approach. If we are just doing it because the books say so, we will probably not persevere. But if we realize that the well-being of our child is at stake, then I am sure we would try our best. The point is, learning to behave differently than we are used to is not impossible, but we need to see the urgency and importance of doing so. Teaching your child is urgent and important—you only have twenty-one years, at the most, to do the job. But most parents fail to see that until their students who have been sitting quietly all along suddenly walk out, and many of them never return.

Gentle Yet Firm

Children need parents as teachers but they hate the feeling of being lectured at, especially once they have reached a certain level of maturity. They usually do not reject what you want to teach them—especially if they find that you make sense—what they repel is the way you teach. If you have the experiences of being taught by a good teacher and a bad teacher, you will know what I mean. The key to teaching serious subjects to your children is finding the right combination of gentleness and firmness. Be firm so you let your children know that the lesson is important, but be gentle so as not to invite rejection. Consider these two ways of responding to the same situation.

> *Tom found out that his four-year-old son had been using swear words at home. He was surprised to find a boy of such young age using swear words that he probably did not even understand. He said to his son, "It is wrong to use swear words because it is rude and inappropriate. They hurt the feelings of other people and you will lose their respect." When his son seemed to understand what he said, he continued, "Remember this, even if people around us are using swear words, we should never follow their bad example because we are smarter and more sensible. I don't want you to ever use swear words again."*
>
> *Jonathan had the same problem with his son. Instead of teaching him why it was wrong to swear, he started to attack his son. He shouted, "I hate it when children swear. You are so stupid. Can't you think of*

any other words to use? Don't ever let me hear one single swear word coming out of your mouth again, do you hear me?"

Do you feel the difference in the tone and feeling of the two responses? Can you see that how you phrase your teaching message is very important? We can deliver the same message to our children in many forms. We can be like Tom and simply state the fact that the child has done something wrong, explain why it was wrong, and what he needs to do to correct his mistake. *The ultimate goal of a wise teacher is to correct the mistake of the child and not to humiliate him.* By being gentle, we give our child the feeling that we still love him, which is hard for them to feel if we shout at them, and by being firm, we are telling our child that even though we love him, a mistake is still a mistake and we will need to make sure that he will not make the same mistake again. We can also choose to deliver the message like Jonathan in a judgmental and critical way. But a teacher who makes his student feel that he is trying to ridicule him more than his behavior justifies will only make the student become defensive and angry. It could be an invitation to a power struggle. A student who is angry with a teacher will never learn from him. If we feel that we are going to react like Jonathan, we may want to take a time-out. You can take a time-out to write down what you want to say and rewrite it if necessary until you are satisfied that you will deliver the right message in a form that your child will be able to hear.

Commanding but Not Harsh

To be in command means that you are able to make your children pay attention to what you have to say, not by twisting their arm, but by being the authority on the subject. Do not confuse this with the authority of a ruler, which works at the submission of the child. Parent-teachers should always encourage their students to participate in any decision making, and thereby learn for themselves. In teaching, we work to inspire and guide, giving children the last say in their decision, as long as the decision is age appropriate and the child is able to pay the price if they've made the wrong decision.

For example, you may want to teach your teenage daughter that calcium intake is most crucial before twenty-three years of age—something you have recently learned. You wish you had known about this when you were a teenager, for if you had, you wouldn't need to worry about osteoporosis now. Though you might be the authority on the subject when you teach your child, you must remember that it is her body and she does have the right to refuse your guidance. You can command a child to take vitamins or mineral supplements when they are younger, perhaps under fifteen years old, depending on how independent they are. But forcing a glass of milk or a calcium supplement down your teenage daughter's throat everyday will be a harsh approach and will only make your daughter focus more on your suppression than on the danger of osteoporosis. However, it will be a totally different case when your child likes to stick his head or his hand outside the car window. This is when you need your ruler hat to safeguard your child.

When a teacher is commanding, she elicits respect as an authority or expert on a subject and the student looks up to her and is willing to learn from her. Excessive harshness will never obtain the same result. To be harsh is to force a student to pay attention to your teaching even when she does not want to learn from you. When your child does not want to learn from you, it is more important to find out why she refuses your teaching than to force her to learn from you.

Dignified and Calm

It is hard to respect someone who we do not look up to, and it is hard to look up to someone just because he or she is in authority or has social status. Famous teachers such as Jesus, Buddha, Confucius, Mahatma Gandhi, and many others are all figures who will be long remembered for what they have done to make this world a better place. However, it is also important that we remember them as people who carried themselves in a dignified and calm way when they pursued their purpose in life. It is hard to respect someone who appears to be vulgar and agitated, even though they can actually be a person worthy of respect.

Since you will put on your teacher hat most of the time during parenthood, it is important to be dignified and calm in appearance most of the time. Your children will respect you for your knowledge and charisma and in so doing, will easily be influenced by what you teach them. If you appear to be a mean and unreasonable teacher most of the time, your look will actually drive your children away from you, physically and mentally.

The best way to stay calm and dignified even when you are facing a difficult situation is to "see" yourself when you are under pressure in front of your children. How? Try to look at yourself in a mirror or set up a video camera. If you do not see a calm and dignified teacher in the mirror or video, you might then also imagine yourself being seen the same way when you talk to your child. You will then understand why your child never listens to you or why he rolls his eyes while you talk. This is not just about how you might look, what is most important is how you feel within yourself. A calm and dignified face is the reflection of a calm and dignified heart.

❧ KNOW YOUR CHILD ❧

If a person can review old knowledge so as to cultivate new realization—such a person can be qualified as a teacher.
(Analects 2.11)

Nobody should know your child better than you. In America, they say, "Father knows best." In China, they say, "No one knows the son better than the father." But can we keep up with a child's constant changes and honestly say that we know our child better than anyone else? The only way to do this is to be observant. Watch his development and review your information about his past. How a child behaves at two-and-a-half is a very good indication of how he will behave at thirteen. If he has always been kind and gentle and he suddenly becomes brutal and vulgar, there must be some problem in his life. It is very important for a teacher to know the student well. By keeping in mind his past and his characteristics, you will actually be much better prepared for your job. Old knowledge could help you to design new teaching methods to make you more effective when you put on your teacher hat.

❧ TAKE A BREAK ❧

Do not converse when eating, and do not talk when retired for the night. (Analects 10.10)

It is important that we are often the teacher, but we must remember to take a break from this role. Mealtime and bedtime are perfect opportunities for us to take off our teacher hat. During these times we should stop teaching, unless the situation absolutely requires us to, and respect the peace of mind of our children and ourselves.

Nowadays, with the busy schedules of everybody in the house, sitting together for dinner is a precious moment. However, many parents waste the opportunity to connect with their children during this time by watching television together or by giving lessons. Meal times can seem like the golden opportunity to teach because your children are a captive audience.

In ancient China, the head of the family, usually the father, always made use of mealtime to lecture his children. It was a time when parents were unquestioned authoritative figures, and children, even adult children, could only listen. No discussion or argument was allowed. Can you imagine the pressure of being "taught" in front of all the family members while your stomach is supposed to work for you while you eat?

Knowing how emotions affect the body system, especially the digestive system, you should try to create a peaceful and warm atmosphere over the dining table. If your young child often complains about stomachaches before his dinner or if your preteen and teen race each other to finish dinner every evening, then maybe you should pay attention to what you usually discuss, or teach, over dinner.

The same holds true at bedtime. Any emotional disturbance will affect they way children sleep; so please do not think of the bedroom as the lecture hall. If your children are young, make sure you spend happy friendly times with them before they sleep. Wrap up the day with big bear hug and a big kiss. No child should go to bed thinking that his mommy and daddy do not love him anymore just because he was a bad boy at the shopping mall that afternoon.

Mealtime and bedtime are bonding time, not teaching time. If a child misbehaves during mealtime or bedtime, take her aside and teach her outside the dining room or bedroom. If the child is young, a time-out will be helpful. If the child is older, reason with her away from the dining room or bedroom. Allocate an area in the house where you can have a "serious" talk with your child that will help you avoid associating teaching time with mealtime and bedtime.

✦ PREPARE YOUR STUDENT FOR THE REAL WORLD ✦

Unlike a schoolteacher whose responsibility is to prepare a student for his next school year, a parent-teacher will need to be there for the child for at least twenty-one years. You do not want your child to do well for just one year; you want your child to do well every year, even after he is on his own as an adult.

You do not just teach your child one subject, you teach him *all* the subjects in life. From walking to driving, you want your child to learn so much from you before he ventures out into the world on his own. Yet a lot of times we forget the big picture and think that we are teaching him just about one particular situation or another. Amazingly, Confucius was completely unlike the ancient teachers who only demanded that students memorize and recite poems and literature. Confucius believed that teachers are meant to inspire and guide students so that they will learn how to think on their own. He always believed that thinking and learning must go hand in hand. Teachers do not only teach a student how to learn, a good teacher also inspires a student to think independently and be able to elaborate on what was taught.

What does inspiration mean in this context? When we think about inspiring our children, we want to get them to be curious about a topic or become interested in learning more about a subject. If a teacher in school only forces a student to memorize a history text without inspiring him to think of the cause and consequences of what happened and how it could be applied to today, he could easily kill the student's interest in history all together.

At home, an inspiring parent-teacher will use her wisdom to show her child a way to look at things from different angles. If, for example, your child is disappointed at losing in his first swimming competition, guide him to look at this failure from different angles. Teach him to reflect on what could have been done to do better than what he did. Did he practice enough? Did he sleep well the night before? Was he nervous during the competition? Tell him that this is a good chance to learn how to handle disappointment by seeing the big picture. The first thing to learn is to be able to analyze and learn from the situation. Inspire your disappointed child to work hard for things he wants to achieve. Teach him that even though he did not get any medal this time, all the effort he put into the training is not wasted. Lead him to see all the "hidden prizes" he has achieved, such as health and fitness, experience in a swimming tournament, friends that he has met through swimming training, and the opportunity to learn about the virtues of discipline, perseverance, and courage. Help him learn more about the virtue of persistence, which will hopefully one day help him to get him the medal of his dreams.

A parent's reaction to a child's failure is very important. Do not hurt a child's feelings by putting him down, while keeping in mind that it is also unwise to spare him the chance to learn from a disappointing experience. The right response from you can inspire and motivate your child to persevere and work harder to achieve their goals.

❧ Teacher is Not Always Right ❧

In striving to be benevolent in your conduct,
do not even yield to your teacher. (Analects 15.36)

Confucius was talking about striving for benevolence, but this could also be extended to other matters in our daily life. We are older and more experienced than our children, but that does not mean that they are always wrong and that we are always right. Give your children the chance to tell you what they think is right. They might not be correct, but by giving them the chance to express their views, you are giving them the opportunity to stand up for their own rights and to explore their opinions fully. At the same time, you are also teaching them the right way to express themselves, to question respectfully, calmly, and clearly. Never let your child be rude to you when he wants to speak his mind, teach him from young age that only by speaking in good manner can they question rules and guidelines set by their parents or teachers.

Many parents simply think that back talk is bad and should not be allowed, period. What they do not understand is that you can actually teach more to a child by letting him question you in a proper way, because you are training him to see things from different angles and to explore his own opinions. Letting a child express his opinion means that you also have to be honest with yourself and be ready to apologize if you find out that you have made a mistake. Do not think that you have disgraced yourself or compromised your parent-teacher role by admitting a mistake. By admitting your mistake graciously, you can actually gain more trust and respect from your child.

In order to determine whether your child has a valid point, it is important that you fully listen to your child's side of the story. Many times children are not very expressive when it comes to their feelings. As a parent, no matter whether you are playing the role of a ruler, a teacher, or a friend, it is essential that you know what your child is really thinking about.

I learned a very valuable lesson from my mentor, Bobbie Sandoz, author of *Parachutes of Parenting*, about how to find out what is on my children's minds. I was told that I had to learn how to listen like a magician. Remember the magician's box where he could pull on just the tip of a colorful scarf and so much more came out? Our job as a parent is to learn how to pull out those scarves one by one until we know exactly what is inside the box. The trick is by probing without judgment or criticism because if we don't, even the tip of the scarf will fall back inside the box. It is only after we know the whole story that we can help our child with his problem.

❦ STUDENTS WHO ONLY KNOW HOW ❦ TO AGREE ARE NOT GOOD STUDENTS

Yan Hui always accepted everything I say without disagreeing with me. This is of no help at all. (Analects 11.4)

Again we are reminded that a student who just agrees with the teacher without reflecting upon what the teacher is talking about is not really learning. Unless you want your child to be a yes-man all his life, encourage him to voice his opinion in a nice way, even if his opinion is different from yours. Confucius considered it the highest level of refinement if a person was able to put aside his own opinion and listen to a different point of view. After much reflection, if the other view makes sense and is reasonable, combine the two opinions and take the middle way for the best effect. If you practice this with your child, he will also learn this from you.

If a child knows that his parents are willing to listen to his opinion, he will have greater respect for them. However, this is not the same as giving children the right to be equals in the family. Young children should never be allowed to make decisions that they are too immature or too inexperienced to foresee the consequences of. In such a situation, tell them that you will have to put back your ruler hat because they are just too young to know the seriousness of the consequences. Be gentle so that it will not feel like you are trying to overpower them. In the role of parent-teacher, you can encourage children to think as they learn, but you will also have to let your children know that you are willing to discuss and compromise only if they are willing to listen and voice their opinion in the proper, respectful way. Make them understand that they are young and full of good and new ideas, but their age and experience will still prevent them from being able to make adult size decisions. Try to accommodate their ideas as much as possible, but explain well, and be firm, when their ideas cannot be followed.

Children are very smart, if they know that they will never be able to "win," they will choose not to talk about the issue. By shutting them out, we will never be able to find out if they genuinely agree with us or if they are just saying so to get rid of us. Be frank with your children about the fact that they are not as experienced in life as you are—I often tell my daughter that she is sensible and mature, but she is still a sensible and mature seventeen-year-old girl—but that you are willing to listen to their point of view. If possible, try to accommodate some of their viewpoint and tell them that they have good reasoning. Do not let your child become someone who thinks that his point of view is always wrong. Put on your teacher hat and teach him how to one day become smarter and wiser than you.

❧ LEARN AND THINK MUST GO HAND IN HAND ❧

If you do not arouse inquisitiveness, you will not be able to inspire;
If you do not make him doubtful, then he will not investigate;
If you show a student one corner of the table, expect him to
describe the other three corners to you. (Analects 7.8)

This is applicable for older children who are more mature. As our children become adolescents, there will be more serious topics that we need to teach them. We no longer need to teach them how to brush their teeth or cross the road. We are faced with topics like discrimination, homosexuality, politics, spirituality, sex, and substance abuse. These are all thought provoking topics and eventually our children will need to make decisions *on their own* regarding these issues.

To be inquisitive is to be curious. Parent-teachers should get students to be curious about the controversial issues we face everyday. If they are not curious, they will not be interested in discussing these issues with you. Why do people discriminate? Is homosexuality a choice? What is the difference between a Democrat and a Republican? What is the name of God? Should one abstain or use birth control? You may be surprised, but most adolescents are more knowledgeable in these topics than you would expect. The reason is because we are just one of the many teachers they have who will influence their decisions. And that makes it even more important for us to discuss these issues with them. It is important for them to know how we feel about these issues, but more important is for us to know how they think.

There will be times that you and your child will hold completely different views on certain issues. Do not try to belittle their opinion or criticize their views, for that will only drive them away from you and deprive them of the opportunity to express their own views. If your child thinks that the name of God is Mohammed and you think His name is Buddha, learn from him about Mohammed and share with him what you know about Buddha. Teaching your child to see things your way does not necessarily mean that he will accept your way in the end. He has every right to accept homosexuality even if you don't, and he can become a Republican even if you have been a Democrat all your life. Nevertheless, don't give up the chance to make him investigate these issues thoroughly before making his decisions.

❦ Hard Work May Not Be a Bad Thing ❧

Confucius said, "Can you really love someone if you do not teach him about hardship?" (Analects 14.7)

This is the genuine meaning behind loving and educating your child at the same time. Nowadays, many parents make it sound like there is nothing wrong with spoiling their children—some are even proud of it. They may think that it indicates that they are able to provide well for their children. But education is not about teaching a child how to enjoy a lavish and easy life; education is about teaching a child how to be strong even when he has to work hard for the things he wants in life.

If you really love your child and want him to be able to survive even when the world around him is in turmoil, you will have to train him well at home. Some people pamper their children because they think they are too precious to feel any pain, physically or emotionally. They worry that by making their child work hard, the child will either dislike his parents or it will damage his self-esteem. In America, when commenting on a child's writing project, we often hear parents say, "Good job, good design, and good idea honey . . . as for the writing, I can see that you have put a lot of effort in it." *But what about the writing?* Parents who are brainwashed about the delicacy of a child's self-esteem give themselves no permission to tell the truth when the child is not doing well with his work.

I am not saying that we should constantly criticize our children, but we need to have a balance here. Children need to know that it is okay if others do not like their work. They need to know how to take criticism graciously and how to work harder to improve their work. If we don't give our children a taste of well-intentioned criticism at home, in a nice way, our children might end up having to learn it the hard way when they need to move out of utopia.

One of the great benefits of encouraging our children to work hard for something is that they will learn how to appreciate the final result. If we simply provide for our children and don't require them to work hard for anything, our children will only learn how to take, and never know how to give. Without knowing how to give back, children will keep asking for more and won't know how to appreciate what they have. To be appreciative is a main key to happiness. It is only when we appreciate what we have that we can be contented and happy.

It does not matter if you are on welfare or a billionaire; your child will need to learn the value behind the good things in life and to appreciate what has been given to him. Too many children today take things for granted and think that their parents owe them a good life. If a child was never made to work for a

98   ❦   THE THREE VIRTUES OF EFFECTIVE PARENTING

minimum wage, how will he learn that he will need to work 214 hours for the computer he got for Christmas?

We all love to see the smiles on our children's faces. Yet, every time we want to be overly generous with our children—with our praise or with money—it is important to remind him that praise and financial achievements are not to be confused with real pride. There is a Chinese saying that says, "To be the man above all men, a person will have to be able to take the hardest of hardship." Hardship to one person might not be hardship to another. The earlier we help our children look problems in the eye and solve them through their own effort, the stronger they will be when they need to face hardships in the real world. Hardship can mean difficulties in all areas of one's life—academic, emotional, financial, physical, personal, professional, or just about anything that is too difficult for a person to handle.

In order to help your children learn how to handle hardship, start with small issues. Make your second grader face his teacher when he doesn't finish his homework instead of lying for your child; make your high schooler take the bus instead of driving him to school; or make your college-bound child work for the extra goodies he wants. All these things help to train your students to deal with hardship. Make them realize that their real pride and genuine self-esteem should be built on character, morality, and strength in life, and not simply from the praise of others or the social status that is bought by money alone.

❦ THE FOUR DON'TS IN TEACHING ❦

Do not speculate, do not demand absolute results, do not be stubborn, do not be self-centered. (Analects 9.4)

It is not easy, or fun, to teach under restrictions, but since we have taken up this meaningful and difficult task, we might as well try our best to avoid these four don'ts, as they might keep us from getting the best results.

1. Do Not Speculate

How often do you speculate about what your child is thinking about when he or she refuses to listen to you? Your daughter might not want to go to dinner at your best friend's house because your friend's husband makes her feel uncomfortable, not because she was trying to be independent. Your son might pretend to be sick because he is afraid of the bullies at school, not because he did not finish his homework. By speculating the motives of our children and not hearing them out carefully, we might be making incorrect judgments based on speculation.

It is hard for parents to resist speculating when we have doubt about what is going on in the life of our children. However, speculation is like worry, it does not help to solve our problems and it will only add on to our mental stress. For example, when your daughter is late getting home or when your receive a call from school that your child is involved in a fight on campus, it is hard to not speculate about what happened and to resist worrying that the worse case scenario might indeed be true. The goal of the parent-teacher under such circumstances is to find out what actually happened, and then teach their children so that they will not repeat the mistake again. Your daughter might be late because she forgot her cell phone and was stuck in traffic due to a car accident on the freeway. She may not have been irresponsible and inconsiderate, as you might have speculated. Your son might have been involved in a fight because some bullies in school attacked him. He had no choice but to defend himself with his Chinese kungfu. As you can see, if you speculate, you might end up teaching the wrong lesson for the wrong reasons. Keep an open mind and do not pass judgment until you know what has happened.

2. Do Not Demand Absolute Results

Do you think that by sending your child to the top piano teacher in town and buying him a Steinway & Sons grand piano he will one day play with the school symphony? A good parent-teacher will understand that there is no such thing as a guaranteed result in the world of raising children. Not being able to become a concert pianist does not mean that you should stop encouraging your child to pursue music. You might be pleasantly surprised to learn that according to Confucius, music is important in the balance of a person. Let your child tell you what he is interested in. Maybe he will be interested in singing, guitar, violin, cello, drums, or just music appreciation classes instead.

Nothing is absolute, including what we had planned out for our children. A parent-teacher can do his best to prepare a child for all kinds of achievements, but the final success still depends on the child himself. A child's talent, interest, and motivation all play an important role in how he will pursue success. As a parent-teacher, you should observe the child's talent and interest before giving him a push in a specific direction, but if the child shows strong resistance or has a good explanation about why he does not want to pursue in what you have planned for him, be flexible and give him a chance to be successful in something of his choice.

3. Do Not Be Stubborn

A good teacher not only teaches, but also listens to the students for their ideas and feedback. Many parents who are immigrants insist that their children should never allow the foreign culture to preside over their native culture. This is difficult and at times frustrating for many children. Parents should not be stubborn when dealing with cultural conflicts. Try to learn about the differences between cultures and have open discussions with your child about your concerns. If you are too rigid with your cultural differences, your child may one day turn against your native culture all together.

For example, sleepovers do not exist in the dictionary of many Asian parents. There was no such thing as a sleepover when I was growing up in Hong Kong. But when my daughter first asked me if she could sleep at her friend's house when she was eight years old, I told her I didn't like the idea of girls sleeping over in friends' houses, especially in the house of a friend that I didn't even know. It was hard for me to understand why they couldn't play until 9 or 10 P.M. then come home for a good night's sleep. I didn't even mind driving her back to the friend's house if there was something else planned for the morning.

At the same time, it was just as difficult for my daughter to understand why I was making such a big deal out of a sleepover party. All her American friends were doing it and it was as accepted in the Western culture as going to the movies. I explained to her that it was not her or even her friend that I did not trust; it was whoever else might be in the house because I don't know the family well. And I didn't even know if their burglar and fire alarms were working. I just did not want to risk sending my little girl out into this real world when I didn't think she was old enough to protect herself from harm.

That wasn't a clash between my daughter and me; it was a clash between her culture and mine. I could have been stubborn and told her that there would be no sleepovers, period. But then that would teach my daughter to be stubborn in problem solving. We finally came to a compromise that she would be allowed to go to the sleepover only if I got to know the friend *and* her friend's parents. On top of that, I also made use of the opportunity to teach her how to be more aware of safety around her in a strange environment. After all, even as adults we will still need to check the fire exit before we sleep in a hotel.

Culture is only one of the factors that might cause a difference of opinion between you and your child. It could also be generation gap, personality difference, or just alternative perspectives. Stubbornness in situations like that will only bring ill feeling and no solution.

It's also important that teachers are not stubborn in their teaching style. Confucius said that teachers should adapt to the needs of each student and that there was no one-style-fits-all in teaching. By that he meant that every student is different and that teachers should be flexible with how they approach their students. For example, if your child is timid and inferior, teach him how to take risks so that he can learn to be more daring. If your child is impulsive and aggressive, teach him how to slow down, so that he can learn to be more patient and careful in life.

4. Do Not Be Self-Centered

If you are a self-centered teacher, you will be teaching your children for the sake of your own liking or convenience.

You might be able to get away with it when they are young, but once they know how to think for themselves, they will notice the selfish motives behind your teaching.

If you are upset with your child when he spills his orange juice because you have to clean up after him or because you hate stains on your beautiful carpet then your anger may prevent you from teaching your child how to be more careful the next time. If you yell or even hit your child you will only make him more nervous. You will not teach him that he needs to watch out for glasses or bottles which might have been placed too near to the edge of the table or that he needs to learn how to slow down his kungfu hands while reaching for the butter.

Many of us allow ourselves to be self-centered in our parenting because we all need to attend to our own needs in life. Problem arises when what we want for ourselves causes us to make the wrong decision with our children. The only way to let go of our self-centered behavior is to center our attention in parenting on the well-being of our children and not on our own well-being. Sometimes it is a very difficult decision when our own needs and our children's needs seem equally important. A wise parent will be able to counter her self-centered behavior with a counter force called sacrificial love. Even though sacrifice suggests giving up something valuable for the sake of others, the sacrificial love of a parent usually will gain us something that is far more valuable to us . . . the love and well-being of our child.

Remember, you are actually wearing your teacher hat all the time when you are with your child. Your child learns from you with or without your permission—consciously and unconsciously. The only way you can win over his other teachers—the TV, the Internet, and pop culture—is to win his respect with your knowledge and wisdom.

Simple Answers to Frequently Asked Questions

WHAT IS A PARENT-TEACHER?

A parent-teacher is someone who assumes the role of teaching his child all that needs to be taught so that his child will one day be well prepared to face the world on his own.

WHY DO PARENT-TEACHERS NEEDS WISDOM?

A parent-teacher needs wisdom because he needs to inspire a child to ask questions and be motivated to learn. It is not wise to teach by forcing your children to follow your instructions without making sure that they understand and agree with what you teach. A teacher also needs wisdom to keep a good relationship with the student. It really does not matter how knowledgeable or wise you are, your teaching will never get through to a student if you have a bad, or even no, connection with your child.

WHEN DO WE NEED TO BE TEACHERS?

We need to put on our teacher hat when there is a decision to be made and we have to teach our child how to make that decision. The difference between a parent-ruler and a parent-teacher is that a parent-ruler needs to have the final say, while a parent-teacher can guide the child to make the best decision on their own, allowing child to have the final say.

HOW SHOULD A WISE PARENT-TEACHER TEACH?

Consider this example. You notice your teenage son has problems controlling his temper when driving. You are very concerned and troubled. A wise teacher will know that it is useless to yell and criticize a young driver for his temperament behind the wheel. This is a very serious problem, but you cannot try to play the role of a parent-ruler, because unless he understands and wants to let go of his road rage, there is nothing you can do to force him to stop such dangerous behavior. Taking away his car will only make him angrier and more dangerous when he gets to drive again.

A wise teacher will teach the child how to manage his anger with benevolence. He needs to be taught how to put on his "benevolence glasses" when someone drives him crazy on the road. He needs to be taught how to see the driver who cut him off as someone who is reckless for a reason of his own, or as someone who never had a chance to learn about the responsibility of a driver. You need to teach him that reacting with rage will only make your son an irresponsible jerk like him. On top of that, a wise teacher will help the young driver see the possible consequences of road rage that he might need to live with for the rest of his life. Last but not least, be kind and loving and remind him of how you love him and that you would be heartbroken if he did something to hurt himself or someone else. A wise teacher leaves his student thinking as he learns how to make the best possible decisions for himself.

Chapter Six

The Courageous Friend:
To Hold Your Child's Heart
Today and Always

WE'VE SEEN THAT THE GOAL OF A RULER IS TO GAIN THE *TRUST* of the child and the goal of a teacher is to gain the *respect* of the child. The goal of a friend is to gain a *connection* with the child. Throughout parenthood, we try to connect with our children in many ways, and in most cases, we connect best with them when we treat them like our friend.

We are a friend to our baby when we play peek-a-boo with him. Later, our baby starts to crawl, and we may crawl on the floor and play like a friend with him. The friend role is the most fun-oriented of the three roles, and yet it can also be the most dangerous and damaging if you befriend your child at the wrong time.

From the very beginning, we need all three of our parenting hats and we need great care to know when to play what role. Can you imagine a parent putting on a ruler hat while crawling on the floor, demanding that the child be obedient and following the way the parent is crawling? Or can you imagine a parent putting on the teacher hat while teaching the infant about the difference between breast milk and bottle milk? Or putting on the friend hat while attempting to persuade a toddler from running into a busy street? These are not very pleasant scenes, are they?

❧ WHEN SHOULD YOU BE THE FRIEND? ❧

I have talked about how a parent can be a ruler when he needs to rule and a teacher when he needs to teach. So when does the role of friend come in? The key issue in determining when to play the role of a parent-friend is again in "decision-making." If a situation requires no decision-making on your part, this will be a time to wear the friend hat and have fun. For example, playing peek-a-boo requires neither of you to make a decision, but teaching him how to walk will require decisions on both sides—you will have to decide how to teach and he will have to decide how to learn or if he wants to learn. For example, going shopping with your daughter requires no decisions but when she wants to buy a pair of designer jeans for $195, it is time to change to the teacher hat. She could either use her own savings or work extra hours or she could pick another pair of jeans that are within her budget.

It might seem complicated in the beginning, but once you get used to stopping to think before choosing your hat, you will soon get into the momentum. Remember, a ruler and a teacher will eventually retire after your child becomes an adult, but a friend will never need to retire and can last a lifetime.

❧ THE ACTIONS OF A FRIEND ❧

When You're a Friend, Only Be a Friend
Zi Gong inquired about how to treat friends and Confucius replied, "Do your best to advise them and skillfully lead them

along the way. But if they are unwilling to listen, then stop—do not disgrace yourself in the process." (Analects 12.23)

You will have to take off your ruler and teacher hat when you are a friend to your child. It is always tempting to demand and to teach when the friend you are dealing with is your own child. Nevertheless, when you treat your child as a friend, he is supposed to be a free person, allowed to make his own decision. That is why it is so important to know when to put on your friend hat. *Think very carefully if the question on hand needs your ruling, your teaching, or simply your friendly advice.*

Friendship requires skill, which is why so many books write about the art of friendship. Through the act of friendship, just as through the act of parenting, we're trying to create a relationship that is beautiful and long lasting. We need the skill to try our best and to persevere despite difficulties. Though we may feel discontented at times, we can never give up. We always have to remember that friends sometimes hold different points of view. You can share your thoughts with your friends, but that is as far as you can go—you can't push for agreement. If you push too hard, you may become anxious and angry. You can sometimes loose a friend by being too adamant.

Be a Helpful Friend
When asked about friends, Confucius said, "There are three kinds of friends who are helpful. Friends who are honest, friends who are forgiving, and friends who are knowledgeable."
(Analects 16.4)

Friends are meant to help each other. In order to be helpful, the first thing you need is *honesty*. If your child wants to go to a movie with you, as a friend, but you are busy with work, be honest with him. Tell him you are sorry but you need to finish your project and that you will make it up to him next week. Do not make up excuses—it's a horrible feeling when you find out that your friend is not honest with you.

When an older child, or adult, comes to you for your advice, be honest with him about how you feel. If there is a dispute, and you think that your child is at fault, be honest about what you think. Don't be judgmental, but be just. Tell him what you think is right and what is wrong without accusations. Telling your child something he likes to hear is not going to help him. It's important, however, that you do not lecture like an authority; don't put on the wrong hat. Before giving your advice, imagine that your child is your best friend and that he is in trouble—this will help you to be more gentle and relaxed. Consider yourself lucky if your child comes to you for advice, you must have done something right along the way.

The second character of a helpful friend is *forgiveness*. If your child ever confesses mistakes he has made or even something he did behind your back, it is a real trial for the strength of your friendship. But remember, he didn't have to tell you in the first place. If he could take the courage to be open and honest with you, then you should also take the high road and show him that you are gracious and forgiving. Yelling at him will only make him feel like he made the wrong choice in coming to you.

Last of all, a helpful friend will need *knowledge*. As your child becomes more independent and mature, becoming knowledgeable about what is happening in their world is very important. Having common topics to talk about will help make the connection between you and your child stronger. One way to find out about your child's world is by reading his or her magazines. Offer them a treat if they go shopping in the supermarket with you and buy them their favorite magazines. Reading their second hand magazines can be quite educational for you. Unfortunately, it usually does not work both ways; it's hard to make children, or young people, take interest in the world of their parents.

Just Between Friends

Do not expose other's plot; do not speculate without investigation; do not be suspicious of what others told to you. If one can do the above, one can be said to be wise and alert with what is going on in other's life. (Analects 14.31)

To have a successful friendship with your child you must prove to him that you can listen without judging and protect his privacy. Reassure your child that what he shares with you will be treated confidentially. There might be things that your child did that you would like to brag or complain about in front of your friends, but unless your child gives you the permission to do so, keep it between the two of you.

Speculation and suspicion are harmful in any relationship. Even as a ruler or a teacher, it is not good for the relationship when you presume to know what's happening without a thorough investigation. This is more sensitive in a friendship, however, because friends should be more open with one another, and true friendship is built upon the total trust of two people. Speculation will sometimes get you to worry about things that never existed. Take courage to investigate the truth and deal with the problem if there is any.

A story was told to me at a parenting seminar that has stayed with me for many years: the speaker asked the audience to imagine driving in a foreign city and getting lost. The person sitting next to us could be calm and understanding, and help us look at the map so that we could work out the way again. Or the person sitting next to us could start to nag about our carelessness, our laziness for not studying the map in more detail, or even start to tell us how she could have done better. A parent is like the person sitting in the passenger seat. How long we can stay in the passenger seat will depend what kind of passenger we are.

Finally, when we're wearing the friend hat it's important to remember to listen to our kids like a best friend, and that we don't react to them too quickly or come to any unfounded conclusions. With our hearts full of benevolence, our minds full of wisdom, and our spirits full of courage the role of a friend will come naturally.

Don't Interfere
*Do not interfere with someone else's duty if you are
not in his position.* (Analects 8.14)

Your child refuses to wear a sweater; you end up staying up all night when he runs a fever. Your child refuses to do his homework; you end up sitting in the teacher's office explaining what happened. It seems like your young child's problems are also your problems, which is why you seem to be interfering with his life most of the time. Yet we should not interfere with problems that belong to our children. We need to learn to ask ourselves if it is our problem or our child's.

For example, do not interfere with young children fighting over toys. If you child wants another child's toy, let him know that even adults do not get to share each other's possessions. Teach him to learn how to find something else to play with in the playground. If someone wants his toy, teach him to feel for the other child (benevolence) but do not interfere and force him to share his toys. In real life how would you like to be forced to share your toys, such as cars, jewelry, computers, and so on? A child will like to share only if he has compassion, not because he is made to.

As your child grows older, his problems will eventually be more of his own. In college, you may not even be allowed to see his grades. It has become his problem if he doesn't do his homework, even though he may still need your help and encouragement. As a teenager, if your child still doesn't like to brush his teeth, your still have the problem of his dental bill, but you should give the ownership of the problem back to him. You are no longer responsible for his toothache. The ownership of problems will affect the way you conduct a friendly conversation with your child. As long as you think that his problem is still yours, you will never be able to be the friend who is caring but non-judgemental. At the same time, it's important that we learn to restrain ourselves from feeling responsible for their problems. Our children will eventually need to learn how to take care of their own problems, unless you want to own them like you own a pet.

Give Your Child Some Space

It is also said, "If in serving your king you are unrelenting, you will bring on humiliation; if in you friendship you are unrelenting, you will find your friends keeping their distance."
(Analects 4.26)

It is bad enough if a friend wants to keep his or her distance from you. But when it is your own child, it can be a painful experience. Yet there are many children who are physically close to their parents and yet distant from their parents in thought.

Everybody needs some space of his or her own. Even a friend who is too insistent will make us feel suffocated. How much more true this is with our parents. That is why we need to have the wisdom to know when to back off so that our children will be able to have the space and clarity to think for themselves. Giving our children space to ponder is another way to counter self-centered parenting. A child who is never given the space to relax, think, make decisions or just be himself will eventually be afraid to have his own space. It will be like having freedom for the first time after a life of imprisonment. Parents who love to run their children's lives will need to consider the damage done to their children and take responsibility for their children's reluctance to get a life on their own.

❧ FILIAL PIETY IN THE ❧ PARENT/CHILD RELATIONSHIP

In the Chinese culture, many grown children have very close ties with their parents. The feelings they have for their parents are usually a combination of respect, fear, obedience, or even dependence. It is quite sad to see how children who are supposed to be independent grownups still cannot break away from the control of their parents. However, if you watch them together, you will notice that many of these parent/child relationships are far from friendly and the children are not at ease with their parents.

Why are some children or adult children not at ease with their parents when they are together? What make them different from those who are at ease with their parents? The answer is the presence or absence of friendship. If an adult child still thinks of his parents as a ruler or a teacher when they spend time together, it is unlikely that they will feel relaxed with them. On the other hand, if the parents can cultivate a relationship that allows a child to be open and amicable, the child will be more at ease.

Disrespectful behavior toward parents is totally unacceptable according to the teaching of Confucius. Absolute filial piety in action and thought was demanded in his day and age. But can today's parents still demand absolute filial piety from their children, even if some of them have actually messed up the lives of their children? Many parents today simply do not deserve filial piety from their children. If you take a look at the statistics of child abuse and neglect, you will understand what I mean. Just like autocratic sovereignty, chastity, or job loyalty, absolute filial piety is a thing of the past, and today's parents should wake up and recognize that filial piety is no longer an obligation for today's young people. Filial piety can only be the natural consequence of their relationship with their children.

Filial piety is expected but not demanded in the West as it is in Eastern culture. In America, parents stress individualism and children are expected to be independent at a certain age. The parent/child relationship is usually friendlier because many parents have been more like a friend to their children when they were growing up. However, being on friendly terms with your children does not necessarily mean that you will definitely have a good relationship with them. For friends can be good friends or not-so-good friends, and if you give your child the total freedom to be your friend when they are young, you also give them the total freedom to do otherwise. After all, friends are on equal bases and are free to do as they please.

If a child had been brought up by a friend who does not take responsibility for his upbringing and does not teach him things that he needs to survive in the world, he will have no trust and respect for this friend who is twenty or thirty years his elder. He will need to learn everything the hard way outside the family because his parent is more interested in befriending him for the sake of avoiding the responsibility of a parent. Eventually, the child will have the maturity to know that this friend of his is just an irresponsible parent in disguise. And if we are looking at the give and take, these parents actually never give, so how could they expect to take back from their children when their children grow up?

Looking at the world around us, filial piety takes on many forms and is based on many things. Tradition, obligation, money, parent/child relationship, these are all factors that will determine how a child will care and provide for his parents when they get old. Tradition and obligation are less observed than before. The third factor is money, and will definitely buy much cosmetic filial piety. But it is only the relationship between a child and his parents that will genuinely make the child the forever friend that will provide his parents with love and care from the heart.

A good parent/child relationship must consist of three elements: trust, respect, and connection. These elements can only be acquired through the appropriate role playing of a ruler, teacher, and friend during the parenting journey.

Simple Answers to Frequently Asked Questions

WHAT IS A PARENT-FRIEND?

A parent-friend is the one whose role is to nurture the parent/child connection so that both the parent and the child will enjoy each other's company. This role gives parents a chance to relax and enjoy their children.

WHY DO PARENT-FRIENDS NEEDS COURAGE?

Parent-friends need courage because they need to let go of their authority and anxiety, so that their "friends" can learn and grow on their own. They also need the courage to stand for what they believe in without imposing their thoughts on their friends.

WHEN DO PARENTS NEED TO BE A FRIEND?

Parents need to put on their friend hat when neither parent nor child needs to make any decision. Parents will need to be a friend whenever their young child needs someone to play with, or when their older child needs someone to talk to. The friend hat is always needed when their child needs a shoulder to cry on. Parents must give their children the opportunity to feel comfortable and secure, with no fear of being criticized or judged, because only then can they be "friends forever."

HOW SHOULD A COURAGEOUS PARENT-FRIEND ACT?

Consider this example. Your fifteen-year-old daughter tells you that her teacher does not like her and is treating her differently in class. You do not like what you hear but want to know more. I once made a *big* mistake telling my daughter that in Chinese culture, if a student wants to learn well, she should respect the teacher and never say anything against him. I heard nothing more from her about the situation, but later realized that I should have put on my parent-friend hat to listen, because teachers do make mistakes and can really be prejudiced and unethical.

Parent-friends will need to have the courage to listen, with active listening skills, even to things they do not like to hear. To be there for a friend is to be there for her without judgment or criticism. It is hard for us to be non-judgmental because we love our children and want to help them every step of the way. However, a parent-friend must learn to let go and listen and acknowledge the feeling of the child. If your child wants you to put on your teacher hat, she will ask for your teaching and guidance.

PART THREE

The Path to Living with Virtue

Parenting with virtue is like fortifying yourself with the inner strength that allows you to withstand all the things that are happening around you and your children. By looking through the eyes of virtue, you will be able to see why parenting has been an uphill battle or smooth sailing all these years. It will also help you to see the past, the present, and predict the future. By cultivating the virtues of benevolence, wisdom, and courage in parenthood, we will be able to be in touch with our own heart.

Many of us have been living with virtues long before we became parents. But how often do we consciously think of these virtues when we face problems in parenting? Virtue and parenting seldom link in our minds because they seem so different. Virtue seems old fashioned while parenting is contemporary. Virtue is for cultivating ourselves while parenting is for raising our children. Virtue seems abstract while parenting is practical. Yet both virtue and parenting are trying to do the same thing—*they both work to improve human relationships.*

It's never too late to practice virtuous parenting, for even though there is nothing much we can do for the past, we still have the present and the future in our hands. Yet, before we can truly cultivate the virtues we desire or change ourselves into the person we want to be, we must take the right road, and learn about the two fundamental elements needed for virtuous living: *awareness* and *reflection*. Both awareness and reflection will help you to see your inner self better, so that you will be more conscious of all the things that you might have overlooked or ignored.

Today's culture in general is consumed with outer life. We spend most of our time chasing after success and recognition, love and security. We are used to looking for satisfaction outside of ourselves. What parents today need to understand is that if we stop chasing results and become still, we will find richness within ourselves that will help us achieve our goals.

Awareness can be unfamiliar to many of us, especially when we don't give ourselves a minute of rest during our busy days. When we become aware of our own thoughts for the first time, we might be surprised with what is actually going on inside and outside of us. By starting to go inside ourselves for answers, we will discover a force we might already possess inside that is more powerful than any parenting technique we might learn. This is the force of our parental love.

Finally, it is important to reflect upon our goals as a parent. According to Confucius, learning and thinking must go hand in hand. He said, *"Learning and not thinking is confusing; Thinking and not learning is dangerous."* If we only study and do not think, we will be easily confused by all the advice we get. If we only think of what to do and do not get educated, we can be dangerous to our children. It is only by learning and reflecting on the knowledge that we can find the right path.

Chapter Seven

Embody Awareness

IN A WORLD WHERE THE OUTSIDE OF A PERSON IS GREATLY emphasized and the inside of a person is rarely appreciated, many people will find themselves disconnected with their inner self. Since both cultivating virtues and making changes require strength from within, we will have to start with the awareness of our inner selves. Awareness is the quality of being awake inside and outside. It is being present in what we are doing and knowing what motivates us to do the things we do.

The topics presented in this chapter are seldom mentioned in parenting books. They do not help to provide you with solutions to everyday parenting problems. *They simply help to prepare your mind and spirit to witness the why, what, and how of your parenting experience.*

To be aware of what is truly going on in your mind is crucial; you will need this awareness as the basis for good parenting strategy. In the *Art of War*, Sun Tze said, "If you know *yourself* and know the other party, you have a 100 percent chance of winning". I am not suggesting that you are at war with your child, but parenting does involves strategy, and sometimes the most important battle to win in parenting is the one inside yourself. You will need to get rid of the bad or unproductive thoughts inside you before you can learn how to become the best parent you want to become. By being more aware of what is going on in your mind and your child's mind, you will find it easier to explore your inner guidance for directions at a crossroad.

Awareness can be enlightening if you see in a way that illuminates things for you, but at the same time, it can also be an uncomfortable experience if you see things that might not be what you want to see.

❦ BE AWARE OF THE PAST AND THE FUTURE ❦

In parenting, what happened yesterday and what is to happen tomorrow both play a very important role in how we handle parenting issues today. Looking back to the past and seeing ahead of what is happening at this very moment allow us to focus on what is more important than just the present parenting dilemma. It gives us the opportunity to remember why we are here in the first place and how our action today is going to affect our—and our child's—days to come.

❦ THERE WAS NO INVITATION ❦

If you invite someone to come and live in your
nation, you have the obligation to treat him well.
(Analects 16.1)

Confucius did not mean children when he referred to "someone" in this quote; he was referring to people whom the kings invited or lured to live in their nation. The meaning, however, is still relevant to parents: if you invite someone to come and live in your territory, you have become the host, and you are obligated to treat your guest well.

No matter if you love or loathe parenthood, you probably started out the same way as all the parents did. I don't mean biologically, but you all started out by inviting your children into your life, without an invitation, without an R.S.V.P. You also did not need the proxy from your child before you could make crucial decisions for him. From his first immunization shot to his last name, you had the right to decide what was best for him from the very start. You also voluntarily provided him with everything that you chose to give him. He never demanded a lullaby or a day at the park (the things you chose to give to a whining or screaming child is another story) and it was you who wanted to work two jobs so that he could attend his dream college.

From the moment your child was born to the day he becomes legally independent, which roughly takes 6570 days, you will be shocked at how much you need to spend on him in monetary terms. If that's not an issue for you, how about all those priceless hours you put in to provide him with your best loving care—the countless nights you stayed awake so that your neighbors, and spouse, could have a good night's sleep? Or what about the innumerable self sacrifices that almost made you lose your own identity? All things considered, it is almost impossible for you to present your child with a detailed list of all that you have done for him when you want to redeem the reward you so deserve.

We often hear parents complain that their children are ungrateful, that they do not act in ways that show gratitude and appreciation. This, again, brings us to a discussion of filial piety. In the ancient Chinese culture, children were obligated to repay their parents with care and obedience. Filial piety was not an option. We talked about absolute filial piety in the previous chapter, but it is also important to be aware of what the term "filial piety" really means.

Filial piety (*Xian Shun* in Chinese is made up of two characters: xian and shun, which have two totally different meanings. Xian means "to love and care for one's parents," while shun means "obedience and compliance." When the two words are put together, they produce the best result. In ancient Chinese culture, adult children, I shall simply address them as children in this chapter, would need to care for their parents with heartfelt respect and compliance regardless of the kind of relationship they had with their parents while growing up.

In today's world, many children still observe filial piety, but most of them will only be able to honor one of the two components. Children who observe xian are the ones who love their parents and take care of their parents in the best possible way. Xian could be expressed by calling your parents just to say "I love you," taking them on a trip, or joining them on a trip to a destination of their choice, or selling your car to buy dad in-home medical equipment. Shun on the other hand, means to act according to the will of the parents without disagreement. In other words, it means to do everything according to the instruction of the parents. It really does not matter if you care about your parents or not, your obedience is all it matters.

Shun is much more difficult to find today because absolute obedience simply does not exist anywhere in a democratic society. Unlike before, we now have permission to stand up for our rights against authorities. It does not matter if you are the president, the boss, the teacher, the parent, or anyone else in a position of authority, you will be expected to be accountable for the things you do. What you do is more important than who you are if you want to be respected by subordinates. Subordinates are no longer obligated to respect and obey their superiors the way they did before.

Today, in China and in America, we still see filial piety being observed by children, but it is no longer an obligation. There are two conditions that need to be met. The first condition is a good relationship between the child and the parent. The second condition is financial dependency, which will only buy shun and not xian, and that is more common in the Eastern family than in the Western family.

Sad as it sounds, parents nowadays cannot just demand filial piety; they will have to work for it. This probably does not sound right to many parents, who would rather cancel filial piety off their wish list than have to work for it. "Why should I bother to work for filial piety from my children? I have Social Security, I have my retirement fund and I have my spouse and enough friends to surround me after I retire. I will love to have my children observe filial piety, but if they don't, I don't really care. I am an independent person." This may be a common enough response among modern parents. But think again. When we speak about filial piety, we are not really talking about a financial provider or a physical caretaker or someone to send us a card on Mother's Day or Father's Day. We are talking about the quality of the relationship we have with a human being that we have brought into this world, who actually shares our genes, and who still loves us after they are financially and emotionally independent from us.

What I am talking about is the very special connection between a parent and a child. He might not have made it to the big name college of your dreams, or he might not have become the concert pianist you so desired, but he is the one who uses his savings to buy you a new bed so that you can sleep better at night, or the one who quietly put a blanket on your 80 year-old-body when you fell asleep watching TV. The love between parents and children is what makes all the pain and agony of parenthood worthwhile and rewarding in its own special way.

Be Aware of the Present

As a parent, we usually take things as they come because there seem to be too many things going on at the same time when we are around our children. We want to love our children; we want to discipline them; we want to teach them a thousand things or more; we want to keep them healthy, physically and mentally; we want to keep them motivated and high-spirited. We want to make our children happy and yet not spoiled; hard working in school and yet balanced in art and music; we want to do the right thing at the right time for the best results. And this is just parenting—what about the other issues in your life, such as health, marriage, finances, work, and what's for dinner?

We are constantly overwhelmed by the things in our lives. We must remember to bring awareness to our inner-self throughout our day so that we can act with clarity. If you have ever traveled on a plane with a toddler, you will probably know the frustration when your child screams and cries just because he can't get out of his seat. You are aware of all the people who pretend not to mind the noise, of the stewardess who tries to fake a smile every time she passes by, or the movie on the big screen that is supposed to be funny, and you certainly are aware of his squeaky scream. You are aware of many things, but you are often unaware of one thing: you are often too tired and embarrassed to be aware of what is going on *inside* yourself.

You may not be aware of your own fatigue and anger, which might not be related to the child, that has caused you to be unreasonable with your two-year-old who just wants to walk around. You may not be aware of the embarrassment and powerlessness that is making you feel annoyed and agitated. If so, then *you have lost your center of inner mastery.* If your mind is not silent, for even just a few moments, whatever you do will be a reaction, and not a response to the situation.

❧ CONFUCIUS AND THE CLARITY OF THOUGHT ❧

Throughout his teachings, Confucius stressed on the importance of thinking. His disciple, Mencius, once said, "With thinking, something is gained. Without thinking, nothing is gained." He also said, "Without thinking, the eyes and ears are hidden from things." If you think about it, thinking actually is more important than learning all the parenting materials presented to us in all our parenting books, because according to Confucius, *"those who learn but do not think will be confused."* Maybe that is why so many modern parents think that parenting is confusing.

Yet thinking can also be a confusing experience if our mind is jammed with too many thoughts. Influenced by Buddhist and Daoist meditation, the Neo-Confucians in the Sung dynasty (960–1279) developed their own understanding of spiritual contemplation and concentration that aimed at calming the mind as a path to sincerity and enlightenment. Many Confucians started to promote a special method called *quiet sitting* or *sitting quietly* in meditation (*Jingzuo*) and believed that it was an effective way to examine one's learning. Quiet sitting is considered to be a technique useful for students to obtain knowledge and self-cultivation. Confucius also expressed that benevolent persons have a preference for quietness and love the mountains (Analects 6.23), and that they are calm and serene. (Analects 7.36) Wise people, on the other hand, love water. This explains why so many Chinese paintings use mountains and water as their theme.

Many parents, especially new parents, will understand that in today's busy and fast-paced world, it is not easy to achieve calmness and serenity. Clarity of thought can only be achieved by stopping and meditating, even for ten minutes a day. It does not matter if you meditate while walking, sitting, or lying down—the goal is to rest the mind for just a little while. Millions of people around the world practice all kinds of meditation. For some, it is a way to relax and enjoy life more fully; for others, it is a serious struggle to achieve oneness with a higher spirit. The reason I want to introduce meditation in here is not for religious reasons—I just want you to be able to learn how to obtain a clear mind when dealing with parenting dilemmas. In this section, you will see how meditation can even help with situations like dealing with a crying toddler on the plane.

We can only be aware of our own thoughts if our mind is clear. You can practice meditation on a plane, in a bus, or in the kitchen (when you're not cooking). All you have to do is to close your eyes and get into a focused state of mind. You will be surprised at what is going on inside you. If you can let your body and mind be at peace, by sitting quietly and meditating, you will see that your mind and body will attune to each other. Now they no longer run in different directions. This harmony between them will help you reach the next step of awareness. It will help you become aware of your feelings, emotions, and moods.

Our responses to a screaming child or rude teenager are usually so distracting that we end up reacting to the situation without clarity of thought. I have seen parents shouting or screaming back at a screaming child on a plane, or in other public places where the child is causing the parents to feel embarrassed. Some parents even try to threaten the child by physical force. Many times, this is the beginning of a real nightmare. After a while, the child may just keep crying, even after he has forgotten what he was crying for in the first place. Very soon, all the other passengers will need to practice meditation so they can stay calm and in control of their own thoughts.

A clear mind will help us recognize our own thoughts and remember the power of benevolence, wisdom, and courage in achieving results. Will we be less angry if we know that our child is as tired and helpless as we are, and that she is afraid of the loud engine noise and is bored of being tied in her chair for the past two hours? It is not an easy task to keep a child tranquil and composed on a plane, but it will help if *we* remain tranquil and composed ourselves.

When our mind is quiet, even when the surrounding is noisy, we can think more clearly, and when we can think more clearly, we will be able to find wisdom to solve the problems. Instead of yelling back at a crying child on the plane, we should be the first one to calm down. Once our mind is calm, then we can consider ways to calm down our child by distracting her with new toys we've kept hidden, entertaining her with puzzles or drawings, satisfying her inquisitiveness by showing her where the lavatory is, or arousing her curiosity by naming the people and things on the plane. It is still no easy task, but at least it is better than sitting there feeling confused and frustrated which only makes children act up more because they can also feel our confusion and frustration.

❧ ENLIGHTENMENT ❧

When we allow our mind to rest, we also allow our mind to open up to the possibility of *enlightenment*—the moment when we suddenly see the light at the end of the tunnel. In parenting, enlightenment is seeing a new and better approach to an existing problem. If our minds are totally jam packed with old thoughts, there is no more space anywhere for new ideas to come in. That is the time we need to quiet down and let go of many of our old thoughts so as to make space for new and refreshing ideas.

Do not feel bad if you try to meditate and your mind does not seem to be as quiet or as "empty" as you expected. Just let the thoughts float in and out of your mind but do not try to control any of those thoughts. For busy people who do not think that they have fifteen minutes to spare, make it just ten minutes. Just close your eyes and imagine yourself floating on water or floating on air. All it takes is one good new idea that enlightens you like a light bulb (just like in comic strips) and you will be sure to find that fifteen minutes everyday.

We have to first cultivate the three virtues of benevolence, wisdom, and courage, and then be aware of any problems in our children and ourselves. Stay calm and clear with your thoughts (even with a screaming child next to you) and wait for the enlightenment that will help you to take parenting to a higher level.

Simple Answers to Frequently Asked Questions

WHAT IS AWARENESS?

Awareness is a state of mind that allow us to be conscious of what is going on in our life; not only what is going on in front of us, but what is going on behind and surrounding what we see everyday.

WHY DO WE NEED AWARENESS?

We need awareness to help us see both the positive and the negative things that are happening between our children and ourselves. It is only through awareness that we can recognize parenting problems that we haven't seen before and how virtue or the lack of virtue can make a difference.

WHEN DO WE NEED AWARENESS?

We need awareness when we feel confused and fail to see the root of the problems we are facing. We need awareness to help us regain our focus on the root of the problems so that we can be enlightened the right solutions to our parenting problems.

HOW CAN AWARENESS HELP WITH PARENTING?

Consider this example. Your four-year-old son spilled his milk for the third time this week. You are getting annoyed and impatient. Shouting and punishing a child for his clumsiness and carelessness will often make him more nervous, which will cause him to be more clumsy and careless. If you keep reminding and accusing a child that he is clumsy, he will truly believe that he is clumsy and will act in such a way. Begin by becoming aware of what you might have done to cause such unwanted behavior. Take into consideration that the child is only four years old and may be trying hard to avoid the accident, even though it may not seem so. If your anger level seems far above a normal level, you might also need to become aware of the genuine reason. Is it the stain on a new carpet? Or is it the embarrassment in front of your friends? Reminding the child to place the glass away from his kungfu hands might help, and teaching him to be aware of the things around him should also be useful.

Chapter Eight

Reflect on Your Goals

IN ORDER TO REACH OUR ULTIMATE GOAL IN PARENTING, WE must reflect—we must go back and investigate how we've been doing so far, and see where we want to go from here. The purpose of this chapter is to help you learn how to harmonize your actions with your goals, because if they are not working in the same direction, you won't enjoy the journey and you'll never make it to your destiny of choice.

❧ REFLECT ON YOUR GOALS ❧

We are all different and it is impossible to generalize and make a single profile of parents. Everyone reading this book has their own combination of personality, education, cultural background, personal achievement, and so many other things, but one thing everyone who is reading this book has in common is the goal to become a better parent.

To reach that goal, we must honestly assess what our current goals are. Many of us—including myself many years ago—are trying to find their dream child. Our child might be fine or even great, but we still think that there are so many things that the child can improve upon. Consciously or unconsciously, we think our child should be more obedient, more sociable, more successful in school, better in piano, violin, soccer, basketball, swimming, drawing, singing, the way they walk, the way they talk, and so on. We must realize that most of our dreams for our children are unrealistic. We need to come up with reasonable goals for them and for ourselves as parents.

⚘ TO KNOW . . . TO LOVE . . . TO ENJOY . . . ⚘

To know is not as good as to love;
To love is not as good as to enjoy. (Analects 6.20)

These eighteen words of Confucius have inspired me to reflect upon how I perceive knowledge. It can be applied to any kind of knowledge, whether it is cooking, singing, swimming, painting, or even what is most important in here . . . parenting. Of all the things we learn how to do in our life, a lot of times we stop moving forward once we know how to do what we want to do. We learn how to draw in kindergarten, we learn how to drive when we are in high school, we learn how to cook when needed, we learn how to sing when all our friends sing karaoke, and then we learn how to parent when we have a baby. Do we just want to *know* how to do all of this? Do we want to *love* to do all of this? Or do we also want to *enjoy* doing all of this?

Don't feel bad if you don't love or enjoy the knowledge you have acquired throughout life, because just learning is praiseworthy. *To Confucius, those who are born with knowledge are of top caliber. Those who become knowledgeable for the sake of learning are a grade below. Those who acquire knowledge when baffled are of the next grade. Those who refuse to acquire knowledge when baffled are of the lowest grade.* (Analects 16.9) In parenting, some people are naturally better parents in the sense that they are more patient, more understanding of human relationships, or more soft-spoken. Then there are people who prepared themselves well even before the first sign of problems in raising their child arise. Then there are people who rush to buy all the parenting books available because things are getting out of control in the house. Then there are those who just don't care.

Parenting is an art, and when comparing a parent to a painter, a parent can either be an artist or just a painter. What makes an artist different from a painter? An artist puts his heart into painting his masterpiece, and despite all of the difficulties he might encounter, he enjoys every stroke of the painting. He can never be sure how the end product will turn out, but he is passionate with his work, for he knows that by putting in his best he will one day be able to produce the best piece of art possible. Artists know what they are doing, love what they are doing, enjoy what they are doing, and never quit. Painters just learn to paint; they don't even need to love painting or enjoy the process. As parents we can be just a painter or we can be an artist. Let's look at another example.

> *Ken had dreamed of becoming a concert pianist ever since he was in the second grade. His dream was to be in a tuxedo and play a grand piano on stage. Unfortunately, Ken was not exactly a talented pianist. His piano teacher loved his effort, but had to admit that he was accelerating much more slowly than many of her other students.*
>
> *When Ken was twelve, he finally got his first chance to perform in a tuxedo on stage. He had won in*

> *a piano competition that was open to children aged six to twelve. Ken was much older than most of his competitors and was far from being a great pianist, but he was an artist who should be awarded for achieving the highest level in "enjoying" how to play piano.*

Ken was not born with musical talent, but he wanted to learn for the sake of learning and enjoying the art. He not only learned how to play the piano, he loved to play, even though he needed to practice twice as hard as others. Most importantly, he enjoyed the experience because he feels his improvement day after day.

Many parents are like Ken, struggling through something that they love to do but have no talent for. When problems arise, they work hard to learn, trying to reach their goals. But many parents have goals that do not align with their ability, and so, in the end, they cannot enjoy what they are doing. If Ken's goal was to play in Carnegie Hall by the time he was twelve years old, he would not have enjoyed his experience playing piano, because his talent and hard work could never have taken him there and he would not be able to reach his goal. It would have been an agony for him. Through this example, we can see how important it is to have realistic and reachable goals.

If you want to learn, love, and enjoy parenting, you must learn to become an artist, because then you will do everything you can to learn how to produce the beautiful painting you desire. You will work hard at overcoming all difficulties; you will persist and persevere even if you have to start all over again when the painting does not turn out right. And all along, you will love what you are doing and will enjoy every moment of the experience. Everyone can be like an artist in his or her parenting experience. The biggest challenge is to be able to reflect and visualize—even in moments when we are in despair—the masterpiece you want to complete by the time your child is an adult. Now, close your eyes and see your child on his twenty-first birthday. This image is your goal—setting the right goal will give you the right direction to pursue and persevere to produce the beautiful painting you desire. Yet, from time to time, you will have to get a reality check to see if your goals are realistic. It's never worthwhile to sacrifice your parent/child relationship for the sake of creating your "dream" child.

To change has never been easy, it takes us out of our comfort zone; it involves new risks and new learning. This is when we need the virtue of *courage* to help take us out of the familiar setting and dare to go for the change; we will need the virtue of *wisdom* to help us to reflect and understand the potential consequences of our parenting style; finally, we will need the virtue of *benevolence* to give us the desire to change. Only by rectifying our mind with virtues will we genuinely know why we want to change, and only by reflecting on why we want to change can we have the strength to do so.

If you follow your heart and make the change, there is still no guarantee that you will win the "Best Parent of the Year" award. But there is one thing that is certain: You will be a better parent that will be painting the picture of a better child.

Simple Answers to Frequently Asked Questions

WHAT IS REFLECTION?

Reflection is an honest review of our actions and our intentions. It's like seeing ourselves in the mirror and getting a reality check.

WHY DO WE NEED REFLECTION?

We need reflection to help us see what we have done and how we got to where we are now. We need reflection to see our goal and our intention clearly. Only with reflection can we allow virtues to help us set the right goal and have the right intention for the best parenting experience we could possibly have.

WHEN DO WE NEED REFLECTION?

We need reflection when we feel that we are lost and do not know where we are going. To reflect on our parenting goal is like finding a destination. It is only after we know where we want to go that we can find the way to get there. If we don't care where we are going, any path can get us there.

HOW CAN REFLECTION HELP WITH PARENTING?

Consider this example. Your twenty-year-old daughter is in love with a young man whom you dislike. You feel lost and discouraged when your daughter does not talk or listen to you any more. This is a case that requires some honest reflection. Why are you so upset with your daughter's lover? Is it because he does not fit into the picture of your ideal son-in-law or is it because you really do not believe that the young man loves your daughter and will make her happy? An honest reflection will let you see your intention.

Once you can make yourself see your intention, you will be able to choose what role to play. If your intention is to gratify yourself, you will take up the ruler role to break them up, so that you can have the chance to find your ideal son-in-law. However, if by being an authoritative and self-centered ruler, you win yourself an ideal son-in-law, it may come at the expense of the happiness of your own daughter. If your intention is to see happiness in your daughter, you will have to be the teacher. With an issue of such significance, to just sit and listen as a friend is not enough. A wise parent will need to carefully teach and guide the child to think and make wise choices on her own.

It is time to put on your teacher hat and guide your daughter to see with clarity all of your concerns. This will not be as easy as taking a toy away from a three-year-old, but a wise teacher should be able to help a young lady who is in love foresee her future, and think carefully about the consequences of her own decisions. A good parent/child relationship is more important than anything else in such critical situations. Never burn down the bridge between you and your child at such crucial moments. Connection is the key. After all the teaching is done, reconcile in whatever way possible and accept her choice and the person she loves. After all, as I mentioned before, teachers can also make mistakes, and students do have the right to choose what is best for them.

EPILOGUE

I have written this book to share my parenting experience, which has been enlightened by the wisdom of Confucius. It is not my intention to invoke or deepen the feeling of guilt or self-blame in anyone, but rather to bring about self-awareness and inspiration to reach for the three virtues of parenting.

For too long, virtues have been neglected, if not ridiculed as old-fashioned or confining. Yet, I have discovered that virtue is, as it was two thousand years ago, timeless and universal and can truly enhance human relationships. By seeing through the eyes of virtue, we actually have more freedom to choose, and more choices to choose from. We can now choose freely between the right path and the wrong path.

In a world where we are so used to instant gratification, the gradual process of self-cultivation could be a challenge for many people. Fortunately, even though the cultivation of virtue is a slow transformation, the payoff can also be in some form of instant gratification. A hug from a "long lost" daughter, unexpected compliance from a deviant son, a parent/child connection that was never there before—all these can feel like instant gratifications for a parent who has taken the time to discover the power of the virtues in parenting. These positive responses from children will generate more loving feelings, which in turn will inspire further progress. It might take a while to get the momentum going, but once we get there, all the gratifications will be multiple and all encompassing. On the other hand, if we try to get there fast but without virtue, we might never be able to get there at all.

In today's culture, we talk so much about changing our body shape or facial beauty. Many work extremely hard to create an "extreme make over" so that they will look better on the outside. Maybe it is time for us to give some attention to the transformation of our inner selves and the cultivation of inner excellence. As a parent, this could be the most important transformation or "make over" of our entire lives.

As with all kinds of transformation, the sooner we start, the less damage there is to mend. But remember, it is *never* too late to better the relationship between us and our children. Even for those of us who have adult children, cultivating virtues will always be the first step to a better and closer relationship with the person who will always be your child.

Confucius believed that a happy and better world started with the self-cultivation of one person. James Vollbracht in his book *The Way of Virtue* pointed out that "if the individual first acquired virtue, he or she could then transform their families, communities, nation, and world . . . and that as more individuals acquired virtue, eventually a virtuous critical mass would appear within the community and culture; a critical mass whose power and force would propel the culture to new heights in arts, science, religion, commerce, and living." It may all seem idealistic, but if you think about it, this grassroots beginning and its effect is the only way we can make benevolence an alternative to the violence so prevalent in this world.

We are responsible as citizens of the world to raise the next generation well, and we cannot do it all by ourselves. We all need to be trendsetters (or "wind" as described by Confucius) who call for the incorporation of virtues in raising our children. The reason is simple. It really does not matter how hard we try to care for and protect our children, because all it takes is one parent who does not teach his child to respect the life of others or one parent who fails to teach her child to be a responsible driver. Our own child could easily become the victim of the next act of school violence or road rage. As we all share the violence in this world, we will also be able to share the love and kindness in the heart of each other.

It is time for parents to join together and embrace benevolence, wisdom, and courage in parenting. Share your discovery with other parents and make a difference. In conclusion, I would like to share with you a wonderful quote from Helen Keller:

> *I am only one; but still I am one.*
> *I cannot do everything, but still, I can do something.*
> *I will not refuse to do the something I can do.*

We may not be able to do everything, but please do not refuse to do the something that you can do for your children.

BIBLIOGRAPHY

Ames, Louise Bates and Sidney Baker. *Child Behavior.* New York: Harper Collins, 1992.

Ames, Roger. *The Analects of Confucius: A Philosophical Translation.* New York: Ballantine Books, 1998.

Chen, Li Fu. *The Confucian Way.* London: Kegan Paul, 1986.

Cloud, Henry and John Townsend. *Boundaries with Kids.* Grand Rapids, Michigan: Zondervan, 1998.

Goldstein, Robin. *Stop Treating Me Like a Kid.* New York: Penguin, 1994.

Huang, Chichung. *The Analects of Confucius.* New York: Oxford University Press, 1997.

Karim, Hajee. *Creating Power.* Publisher unknown, 2002.

Lau, D. C. *Confucius: The Analects.* London: Penguin Books, 1979.

Leys, Simon. *The Analects of Confucius.* New York: Norton & Co., 1997.

Moore, Jennifer Oldstone. *Understanding Confucianism.* London: Duncan Baird Publishing Ltd., 2003.

Sandoz, Bobbie. *Parachutes for Parents.* Chicago: Contemporary Books, 1997.

Severe, Sal. *How to Behave so Your Children will Too.* New York: Viking Books, 2000.

Simpkins, Alexander and Annellen Simpkins. *Simple Confucianism: A Guide to Living Virtuously.* Boston: Tuttle Publishing, 2000.

Vollbracht, James. *The Way of Virtue.* Atlanta: Humanics Trade Group, 1995.

Waley, Arthur. *The Analects of Confucius.* New York: Vintage Books, 1989.

Wolf, Antony. *Get Out of My Life but First Could You Drive Me & Cheryl to the Mall: A Parent's Guide to the New Teenager.* New York: Farrer Straus Giroux, 2002.

Yutang, Lin. *The Wisdom of Confucius.* New York: Random House, 1994.

Photo by Laurie Callies

ABOUT THE AUTHOR

Shirley Yuen applied her study of Confucianism and Journalism to parenting by "investigating the truth" (*Ge Wu Zhi Zhi*). She graduated from the University of Southern California with a master's degree in Journalism and has spent the last 16 years researching and studying parenting and child development. She currently works as a speaker to schools, child welfare organizations, and parenting groups. She has two children in college and lives in Honolulu and Los Angeles.